Dawn Ebert
852-4910

Pg 30 The Our Incredible Journey
to find the new home
God has for us which comes
from the effects + results of
our lifes story. Pg 44

Praise for
To Be Told

"This is a book worth reading. Because this is a journey worth taking. To know who you are. To make sense of your life. To discover the role God is giving you in his story. That is a life worth living. Thank you, Dan, for a wonderful book!"

> —JOHN ELDREDGE, best-selling author of *Wild at Heart* and *Epic: The Story God Is Telling and the Role That Is Yours to Play*

"Dan Allender's books brim and sizzle with stories—many poignant, many hilarious, and many both. This book takes us to the deepest stories of all— our own stories, the ones that haunt when they are kept secret and liberate when they are told and known. *To Be Told* is a treasure to be read slowly and with your closest friends."

> —BRIAN MCLAREN, pastor and author of *A Generous Orthodoxy* and *A New Kind of Christian*

"The concepts in this book have helped define my life in magnificent ways. By further exploring my own story, I discovered God's story. And it is a beautiful picture of clarity, purpose, knowledge, and celebration. Thank you, God, for giving us Dan Allender."

> —KATHY TROCCOLI, singer, speaker, and author

"When Dan Allender tells stories, prepare for three things: laughter, tears, and piercing insight. Allender is a great storyteller because he knows that stories are for redeeming, not just for passing the time. This book, about story and full of stories, will help you find your own place in the greatest story ever told."

> —DANIEL TAYLOR, author of *Tell Me a Story: The Life-Shaping Power of Our Stories*

"Dan Allender confronts us with the truth that we are storied people, that each of us is a story, and that we are in fact writing our own stories. With humor and grace, Dan invites us not only to write our stories metaphorically but literally to begin to write our stories. He promises that in so doing we might just possibly find God, with whom we are coauthoring our stories, and we might actually connect in vital and healing ways with ourselves and with each other."

—STANLEY J. GRENZ, author of *Rediscovering the Triune God* and *A Primer on Postmodernism*

"In *To Be Told,* Dan Allender creates an intimate, safe place where we feel free to join in the discussion and dive, with a sort of careless courage, head-first into our own stories. I wept as I rediscovered the sacred and divine in my own story, and began to find the connections between my own story threads, an understanding of my long-aching need to be heard, and the glimmers of a holy redemption."

—RENEE ALTSON, author of *Stumbling Toward Faith*

"Dan Allender calls us to recognize that our lives, which often seem random, have a brilliant, divine coherence. Under his expert tutelage we discover how to discern God's hand on our lives and how to tell the story to ourselves and others."

—TREMPER LONGMAN III, author of *How to Read the Psalms* and coauthor of *The Cry of the Soul* and *Bold Love*

to be **told**

KNOW YOUR STORY • SHAPE YOUR FUTURE

Dan B. Allender, PhD

WATERBROOK
PRESS

TO BE TOLD
PUBLISHED BY WATERBROOK PRESS
2375 Telstar Drive, Suite 160
Colorado Springs, Colorado 80920
A division of Random House, Inc.

Details in some anecdotes and stories have been changed to protect the identities of the persons involved.

ISBN 1-57856-948-6

Library of Congress Cataloging-in-Publication Data
Allender, Dan B.
To be told : know your story, shape your life / Dan B. Allender.— 1st ed.
     p. cm.
   Includes bibliographical references.
   ISBN 1-57856-948-6
  1. Christian life. I. Title.
   BV4501.3.A46 2005
   248.4—dc22

                                                              2004022768

Printed in the United States of America
2005—First Edition

10 9 8 7 6 5 4 3 2 1

To:
Jo Ann Bope Allender

Being of My Beginning
Life Giving
Love Offering
Mother

Contents

Acknowledgments

There are many makers of this book, just as there are many who have written my story. To fail to name is not in this case the same as a failure to remember. To name is to confess the indelible mark of gratitude, and to these kind souls I say:

Matt Baugher, my agent: What laughter, wisdom, and sweet care you endlessly offer. Thank you.

Ron Lee, my editor: Your kindness and erudition weave a stronger voice than I can offer on my own.

Don Pape, my publisher: Bold man, you do not live finally for the dollar but for the hint of divinity.

Linda Busse and Samantha Graham, bosses of the office: Your departure is an ache and your care a provision of some of the greatest goodness of my life.

Allyson Baker, wise guide: By your deep belief and care for my soul, you've called me countless times to fly to the face of God.

Colleagues and board at Mars Hill Graduate School: What a wonder of a story we've been called to create! Thank you for the ride of my life.

Sunset Presbyterian Church, Portland: What gracious hosts to let me speak this book before it was fully formed.

Esther Project: Women of valor, partners in crime, wise and dangerous friends, thank you for reading and calling me to participate in a story beyond my dreams and fears.

Elizabeth Turnage: Oh, what a surprising and gracious gift of writing each other's lives for glory.

Tremper Longman III: As always, the tap on my shoulder is the beginning of all good stories. You've watched my back from the beginning, and may our loyalty outlast our departure.

Annie, Amanda, and Andrew: Children of promise, you are gifts of hope that keep me waiting to see how your stories evolve.

Becky: All ways. Always love in love, above all others, never the same. Always more than I can imagine, always more than I can fathom or desire. There is no story outside of you, no reason beyond your Creator. I praise the One who made you and who created me to be inextricably bound to the glory of your story.

what's your story?

If I asked you to tell me your story, what would you say? Would you mention the pressures you're facing at work? Would you talk about where you went to college? Would you tell me it's none of my business?

Everyone has a story. Put another way, everyone's life *is* a story. But most people don't know how to read their life in a way that reveals their story. They miss the deeper meaning in their life, and they have little sense of how God has written their story to reveal himself and his own story.

If you don't think such things are important, consider a conversation I had recently with a friend who was weighing a career move. He showed me a list of pros and cons. There were an equal number of problems and benefits no matter what he decided—whether he changed jobs or stayed where he was. "If the list is weighted according to my values and dreams," he observed, "it's a dead heat. I might as well flip a coin."

But my friend was overlooking his own story, the one thing that would give him direction in making this decision. He hadn't considered God's authorship of his life. He was aware of God's authority but not of God's ongoing creative work in his life—and in all our lives.

"Which choice allows you to live your life most consistently with how God has been writing your life story?" I asked.

My friend had no idea what I was getting at. So I asked him if he'd ever studied his life to see what story, what themes, and what plot God was writing his life to reveal. He still looked at me as if I were from outer space.

"Why would I study my life?" he asked. "I was there as everything happened, so what is there to study?"

This is a bright, honest, good man who is sensitive to God. He listens well to his wife's heart, and he is intentional about doing the right thing in countless areas of his life—health, finances, time with his kids, and spirituality. But he saw no value in reading his own story.

Most of us have spent more time studying a map to avoid getting lost on a trip than we have studying our life so we'll know how to proceed into the future. When we're preparing to make significant decisions, why will we study a stock report but fail to look at our own story? Why will we read various op-ed pieces to help clarify our views on a controversial topic but ignore our own past, which helped form our most important views? If we're taking a course, we're willing to study books that bore us to pieces, but we won't take time to review our own life, which holds answers about God and our selves that will thrill us, amaze us, and sober us. We read and study a great variety of sources and spend time researching our options in order to live in the right direction. But seldom do we approach our own life with the mind-set of a student, eager to learn, gain insight, and find direction for the future.

We habitually push aside the one thing that can clarify not only how we got to where we are today but also where God is leading us tomorrow and beyond. Our own life is the thing that most influences and shapes our outlook, our tendencies, our choices, and our decisions. It is the force that orients us toward the future, and yet we don't give it a second thought, much less a careful examination. It's time to listen to our own story.

WHAT YOUR LIFE REVEALS

If you stick with me awhile, we'll take a close look at four core issues that are of crucial importance to you—even if you don't yet realize it.

First, God is not merely the Creator of our life. He is also the Author of our life, and he writes each person's life to reveal his divine story. There never has been nor ever will be another life like mine—or like yours. Just as there is only one face and name like mine, so there is only one story like mine. And God writes the story of my life to make something known about himself, the One who wrote me. The same is true of you. Your life and mine not only reveal who we are, but they also help reveal who God is.

Second, neither your life nor mine is a series of random scenes that pile up like shoes in a closet. We don't have to clear out old stories to make room for new ones. Both your story and mine have unique characters, surprising plot twists, central themes, tension and suspense, and deep significance. Each is an intriguing tale, and neither is fiction. Our story is truer than any other reality we know, and each of us must discover the meaning of what God has written as our life story. In our story God shows us what he's up to and what he wants us to be about.

With the third core issue, things start to get exciting. When I study and understand my life story, I can then join God as a coauthor. I don't have to settle for merely being a reader of my life; God calls me to be a *writer of my future.* He asks me to take the only life I will ever be given and shape it in the direction he outlines for me. I am to keep writing, moving forward into the plot that God has woven into the sinews of my soul.

And fourth, there is the necessity and blessing of telling our story to others. To the degree that we know God and then join him in writing our story, we are honored to join others in the calling of storytelling. God, of course, is the Master Storyteller. His self-revelation is captured in a sweeping narrative and then given to us in the Book that grips our heart and captures our soul. God also creates a story with each person's life—a story that we are meant to tell. And since we are called to tell our story, we are also called to listen to the stories of others. And since we are to tell and to listen, then even more so we are called to encourage others to know and tell and listen to God's story as well as their own.

God is calling us to fully explore, to fully enjoy, and to fully capture the power of the Great Story, the gospel. And we are to invite others to immerse themselves in the Great Story.[1] One way we do this is by listening to our lesser stories and then telling them to others.

Listening to Your Story

Do you ever feel that you're stuck, just going through the motions, not hearing from God, and not feeling any passion about your life? It's easy to land there if you're not listening to your story.

God writes our story with great passion and desire, and he reveals our own passions and desires as we read and listen to our story. So I was saddened to see my friend about to make a huge life decision without first asking: *Who am I? What about God am I most uniquely suited to reveal to others? And how is that meaning in my life best lived out?* My friend wasn't listening to his own story to gain direction for his decision about the future.

I'm grateful that he accepted the counsel of a self-confessed fool and answered a series of questions that I asked him to consider. You will be asked to answer the same questions as you read this book. To answer these simple questions, you must study your own story. You must listen to the heartache and hope that are etched in the narrative of your life. And you must find the meaning God has written there.

I asked my friend to join God in writing the next paragraph and then the next page of the story that is his life. I'm asking you to do the same. Allow others to read and edit and critique and join in the glory of the great story God is telling through you. Your story helps reveal the Greatest Story, the story that God is telling about himself. God intends for each of us to live for a greater glory, and a greater story, than our own.

So take seriously the story that God has given you to live. It's time to read your own life, because your story is the one that could set us all ablaze.

WRITING YOUR STORY

In addition to listening to your story, you need to write your story. At the very minimum, this means you need to name your story. And naming means saying far more than "My parents largely ignored me, and I felt abandoned." Or even "I had a happy childhood. I never knew life could be so hard until I grew up."

In my work as a psychotherapist, I often hear these statements. But when I ask the person to narrate, to tell the stories of life that brought him or her to make these statements, I usually get nothing more than a stare. I might as well ask the person to tell me the meaning of $E=MC^2$ and to do so in Farsi.

If we can admit the pain and loss and injustice of the past, then why is it so difficult to tell about the day just prior to each incident that marked our life with shame or anger or emptiness? Why can we not decipher the themes of our life up to that point? And what about the setting—the sounds and words and sights and smells—of each damaging incident?

We know our stories very well. We just don't yet know how well.

Your story has power in your own life, and it has power and meaning to bring to others. I want your story to stir me, draw me to tears, compel me to ask hard questions. I want to enter your heartache and join you in the hope of redemption. But your story can't do these things if you can't tell it. You can't tell your story until you know it. And you can't truly know it without owning your part in writing it. And you won't write a really glorious story until you've wrestled with the Author who has already written long chapters of your life, many of them not to your liking.

We resist telling a story we don't like, and we don't like our own stories. But consider this: if you don't like your story, then you must not like the Author. Or conversely: if you love the Author, then you must love the story he has written in and for your life.

Let's engage the Author of our story so we can enter into the joy he holds before us if we live out our story for the sake of others. If we come to know our story and then give it away, we will discover the deepest meaning in our lives. We will discover the Author who is embedded in our story, and we will know the glory he has designed for each one of us to reveal.

It is toward this good end that we now set out.

part 1

your name and your story

chapter one

the tale to be told

Reading Your Life as God Has Written It

I wonder what sort of a tale we've fallen into?
SAM, *The Fellowship of the Ring*

"Yes, that's so," said Sam. "And we shouldn't be here at all, if we'd known more about it before we started. But I suppose it's often that way. The brave things in the old tales and songs, Mr. Frodo: adventures, as I used to call them. I used to think that they were things the wonderful folk of the stories went out and looked for, because they wanted them, because they were exciting and life was a bit dull, a kind of sport, as you might say. But that's not the way of it with the tales that really mattered, or the ones that stay in

9

the mind. Folk seem to have been just landed in them, usually—their paths were laid that way, as you put it."[1]

That's an accurate description of life. God is constantly writing our story, but he doesn't send us the next chapter to read in advance. Instead, we all read backward—finding the meaning in our stories as we read what God has already written. Life is a story that unfolds in such a way that we can't see very far ahead. We don't know the final outcome, or even the next plot twist, until we're there in the middle of it.

As Sam says to Frodo in *The Fellowship of the Ring:* "I wonder what sort of a tale we've fallen into?"

"I wonder," replied Frodo. "But I don't know. And that's the way of a real tale. Take any one that you're fond of. You may know, or guess, what kind of a tale it is, happy-ending or sad-ending, but the people in it don't know. And you don't want them to."[2]

I remember the first time I read those words: I felt a chill, an irrevocable shudder. I've never had the patience or wisdom to read J. R. R. Tolkien's famous trilogy all the way through, but I saw each of the movies twice. Still, those words—even when they're read out of context—are haunting.

The powerful truth of Frodo's observation arrived in an e-mail from a dear friend who has suffered with me through the many years it has taken to bring a young graduate school into existence. The years have thrown us both into loss, exhaustion, confusion, betrayal, setbacks, undeserved grace, and the presence of God. If I had known in advance what this journey would require, I never would have signed on. However, I don't regret for an instant the price it has exacted, when I consider what I have experienced, become, and am led to be.

As Frodo says, the people in the story don't know what type of tale it is. We can make a guess, but only the Author knows the outcome.

What Sort of Author
Do You Have?

You are a story. You are not merely the possessor and teller of a number of stories; you are a well-written, intentional story that is authored by the greatest Writer of all time, and even before time and after time. The weight of those words, if you believe them even for brief snippets of time, can change the trajectory of your life. In fact, those words will call you to a level of coauthorship that is staggering in its scope and meaning.

✓ God is my Creator, and I am his creation. When I make this statement, I hardly ever meet with any objections. Adherents of all great monotheistic religions believe God is our Creator. When we consider God to be our Creator, we place ourselves in a position for comparison to other entities. We are part of his creation as are the stars, the sea, centipedes, and squash. Furthermore, we are beings who bear the mark of his being. Those who hold to the authority of Genesis 1 say that humanity is marked with a uniqueness that sets us apart from all of creation, no matter how great or small, odd or glorious. Man and woman are made in the image of God.[3] Humankind is the apex of creation.

God is the Potter, and we are the clay. Even the word *human*—derived from the Latin word *humus,* meaning "dirt"—shouts loudly about our origin. We are dirt. The name Adam (Hebrew, *'adama*) means "red," the color of clay. God shaped, molded, and formed us to reveal something about himself. He is a Being who loves to reveal and who invites us to join the process of revelation by calling us to ask, seek, and knock. God always intended for his children to join him in completing creation. We are not inanimate entities that merely reveal glory but living stories that are meant to create glory.

What Sort of Characters Populate Your Story?

Perhaps the best way to start getting in touch with your story is to consider the various characters—both major and minor—who make an appearance. I know the power of this statement from personal experience. To be specific, I must acknowledge one of the most important characters in my own life because my story is buried with him. This pivotal character is my biological father.

My story begins when I was nineteen years of age. I was looking through a box of photos stored in my mom's closet, and I found a family portrait. It was a picture of my mom, a young boy (me) of about three, and a man I'd never met. The look of his face haunted me.

There in front of me was my face as a three-year-old right next to a man who possessed my face as it would look when I turned thirty. This discovery was as odd as falling through a hole in the ground and ending up in a kingdom where the Queen of Hearts is shouting, "Off with his head!"

I took the family portrait to my mother, who was working in the kitchen. "I know that is you, and I recognize myself, but who is that man?" I asked. She seemed unfazed, as if I had asked whether she wanted me to take out the trash. She replied, "It is your father."

I felt stupid. Not unintelligent, but dumbfounded. It was like falling off a ladder. To tell someone about falling off a ladder takes time to narrate. But to actually fall off a ladder takes nothing more than a misstep immediately followed by a plunge. The fall takes no time at all. Yet, like any traumatic event, such a fall takes forever. Time slows down, and the thud comes well before the fall is even registered.

Standing in the kitchen with my mother, I fell and hit within a millisecond, but it has taken me three decades to finally name what that means.

I pointed to the man my mother identified as my father. "You mean the man sleeping upstairs?" She said, "No, he is your stepfather. The man in the picture is your biological father."

I asked many more questions and heard enough to know that I couldn't bear to hear any more. In an instant my life had become both a farce and a great mystery to me. I had discovered a truth that seemed more bizarre than any lie I had ever told. I was not myself. My name was not my name. My face was not the face of the father who had raised me, but of another father, a man who had been lying dormant in a shoe box. That night I took enough LSD to scatter my mind to the wind, hoping the fragments of my life might blow away like the ashes of my torched name.

That was thirty-one years ago, and it's only in the last year that I have asked: "Who is my father? What is my name? Why is my story written with such dark and thick strangeness? Do I really believe that God not only wrote my story but that he also loves my story? What might I become if I believed that God is both my Authority and my Author? What does it mean to coauthor my story with God? Is he the Author, and am I the translator to another language?"

Do any of those questions even matter?

I know one thing for certain: I need to meet my father. I need to find out where he is buried and learn if I have any cousins or other relatives still alive. I need to know my story. And there is a reason for this quest. It is a profound and central theological question: Who am I? And what does it matter that I am "me"?

I'm not advocating a return to the sixties' quest for self-identity and self-fulfillment. This is a search not for fulfillment but for narrative. It is not enough to find a self. Instead it is imperative to search for one's story. It is not I who must be found. Instead it is God who is to be found. He waits—quietly, passionately, and winsomely—within my story. All I must do is ask, seek, and knock.

Again, I can't know my story unless I know the characters who have shaped my character. I need to know who shares the stage with me. The cast is sometimes obvious—our parents, siblings, spouse, mentors, abusers, and friends. But sometimes an important role is played by a grandparent we barely knew or a person, a family secret, who stands in the shadows offstage.

We are defined by the people in our life. The characters enter the stage, speak their lines, and then either stay or depart. We are not the most important character in our own story, but we are almost always on the stage. And we will not truly know the Author of our story, the meaning or the plot of our story, until we know all of the primary and peripheral players on our stage.[4]

WHAT SORT OF PLOT DOES YOUR STORY HAVE?

Aristotle defined story as having a beginning, a middle, and an end. Some other pundits have reminded us that it may not necessarily follow in that order. Still, Aristotle's simple structure defines the nature of any story.[5] It has a first line, an opening chapter, a first act, and this beginning seldom coincides with our birth. Our story begins with the characters who gave us birth, including their past relationships with their parents and issues such as success and shame; power and abuse; love, loss, and addiction; heartache and secrets; and family myths. Our birth is a beginning, but we owe our existence to the generations that came before us. Our beginning, which took place before we were born, signals some of the themes that will play out in our life.

I was born after my mother had nine miscarriages. I didn't learn this until after I discovered that the father who raised me was not my biological father. I was a wanted child. I was, indeed, most wanted. And I was an only child. There was simply no more room in my mother's womb—or heart—to risk the exhaustion and despair of another embryo. I was it.

Even if no other dimension of my beginning were named, this one would tell a great deal about the dynamic that was played out between my mother and me. She is a warrior. She is a tough, resilient survivor. But when I was growing up, she depended on me and looked to me as her reason to exist. I was more important than her marriage and even her life. This is a portion of my life's plot.

Both your plot and mine are formed in the circle of relationships into which we were born. Our plot includes the age or unique situation at the time of our birth. It also involves the tension of the tragedy that is our lot inherited from the Fall. A plot is a thematic merry-go-round that circles in and out and around the curse of creation and makes movement from the beginning to the end a ride on a roller coaster. Remember, the narrative unfolding of beginning, middle, and end does not always march in sequence.

In many ways, the plot of our life is the story of humankind. It is about how we came to be who we are (Creation), how we lost ourselves (the Fall), what it means to discover the name God has written for us (redemption), and how the ending of our story reflects the great consummation of God's story (his coming). Our plot is an encounter with the heartache and dreams and desires related to our personal tragedies—the events of our life that occur between fall and redemption and, ultimately, glorification.

Tragedy and Tension

Every life is under the curse, a consequence of Adam and Eve's turning from God to embrace the delectable lie of evil. The most dramatic moment in the history of humanity, other than the *Second Adam's* faithful surrender to the Cross, thrust humanity into the course of sorrow, loss, and harm. Every woman will labor with loneliness; every man will struggle with futility. It is written into the plot of the earth.

As a result of Adam and Eve's folly, we all have been cast east of Eden. We live as aliens who know we are not at home and whose plot always involves efforts to rise above the tragedy of our condition. We seek a way to return to an Eden that will bring resolution and peace. We are looking for our Eden and the intimacy we would have known with our heavenly Parent had we not disobeyed. At the same time, we are trying to make sense of the earthly parents we have been given. And we are simultaneously trying to understand our time, face, and name.

In other words, we are trying to make sense of our story.

One wise person said anonymously, "Adversity introduces us to ourselves." And adversity comes in too many forms to number. It is the diagnosis of cancer that throws us face to face with mortality. Seeing the real possibility of death creates a newness and drama and calls most people to rewrite the story they previously had assumed was the dominant plot of their life. The introduction to ourselves can also come in the upheaval of unwanted change—tragedy that disrupts the status quo and compels attention, focus, engagement, and choice. This change drives us to write what we really want to say, because we have only a few blank pages left and little ink in our pen.

Even when tragedy has nothing to do with physical death, it still involves a form of death in the shattering of *shalom,* or harmony. A divorce is a death. Sexual abuse is a death. Betrayal in a relationship, the loss of a job, conflict in a marriage, an auto accident, an illness, loss of meaning or hope or joy—all are forms of death. In the Bible God makes it clear that rebellion results in death. Death lies at the heart of all tragedy and at the core of every personal narrative.

It is death that evokes tension, an essential element of any narrative worth telling. A plot without tension is flat line, a life with no rises, no dips, no anima. Life, by definition, involves tension. Even the couch potato, the average adult who watches 4.2 hours of television every day, is drawn to tragedy and tension in the stories of others. This attraction is the reason we are so bound to sitcoms, pulp fiction, reality TV, and water-cooler gossip. We would die without the thrill, uncertainty, and passion of tragedy and tension.

Tension is living in the gap between certainty and uncertainty. We always begin with what we know and are irresistibly drawn to what we don't know. We are inveterately curious. We are wired to grow, and all growth stretches us beyond our comfort level. Comfort is the absence of tension; growth requires a swim in murky, dangerous waters. We want adventure, but not without assurances that we will suffer no harm when we take risks. We want danger and excitement, but only as long as they come with a money-back guarantee that everything will work out before the game is finished.

But life isn't like that. There are no safe risks. There is no growth that comes with a guarantee of success. Tension is the medium in which we breathe every day.

The Tragedy of Your Story

No matter how predictable you perceive your life to be, the possibility for tragedy is always there. A child may be pedaling his bicycle to the safely enclosed community swimming pool when he is struck down by a drunk driver. Tragedy will inevitably deliver its goods to our door. It's life.

Tragedy gives movement to our story as we attempt to change or give meaning to our taste of death. Yet we are always much more than our tragedies. Each one of us is unique. We have a different name, face, and body from any other person who might be grappling with the same tragedy. Two young girls might have lost their fathers in a drowning accident. Both face tragedy, but do they share the same kind of tragedy? And will both of their lives be marked by that violent intrusion? The answer to both questions is yes.

But what if one girl had been sexually abused by her father while the other girl had a sweet and gracious father? Our story is always marked by the unique plot we have been given. As we engage the inevitable suffering of life, we develop patterns of response that eventually become themes not only of how we relate to our world but of how the world relates to us.

A pattern for the sexually abused girl who loses her father might be to cut herself off from others and live a fantasy of a new and better life. Due to her past abuse, she is relieved that her father is gone, yet she is utterly alone because he was the only person who pursued her. In her ambivalence and flight from harsh reality, she might turn to books to find relief, meaning, and hope. As she wrestles with her tragedy, she will develop certain patterns of response—such as isolation, inward reflection, habits of reading or writing—that mark her life.

This girl will not grow up and find her husband at a monster-truck rally. It is also unlikely that she will gravitate to a degree in engineering. Patterns set up themes that begin to define who we are, and that definition often creates new experiences that validate who we are.

To understand our story, we need to know our tragedies, and as we learn them, we will catch a glimpse of how we currently manage tension. Repetitive patterns have become themes in our lives over time, themes that impose structure on us even when a surface evaluation would tell us that these themes are nothing more than personal preference or desire. We are not wholly our own, nor are we exclusively the result of what has happened to us. No wonder reading the plot of our lives is so difficult.

Yet it is in the plot where we will find meaning. It also is the only part of our story we can rewrite if the trajectory of our life is not as we desire. I can't change my tragedies, nor can I really eliminate (fully) the characters in my story, but I can write a new plot. To do so requires reengaging the tragedies of my life with new patterns, thereby developing new or additional themes that mark who I am both as a coauthor of my life and an editor of my future. Doing this marks me as a character in a larger story, a player who furthers the plot development while living in the real world of tension and tragedy. To know our plot is the first step in changing it.

What Sort of Ending Are You Writing?

An ending can be either good or bad. There are excellent novels that held my attention and moved me for hundreds of pages only to end in a way that made me regret reading the story. Sadly, the same can be said of many "good" lives. It is not enough to live well and serve humanity, care for your family, and lead an honest life. A good ending involves much more than making a moral point or teaching a lesson. And a good ending is more than the resolution of the tragedy and tension of an exciting plot.

A good ending doesn't have to be safe or nice. It only has to bring the story to fullness. It is not much different from dessert. An excellent meal, wonderfully prepared and served, is often followed by the least necessary part—dessert. Dessert is often highly caloric and nutritionally bereft. Dessert is the finish, the final indulgence—as is any good ending to a life. Endings are meant to be a sensual, wild fullness of all that came before. And, as you think of endings, it's important to understand that they have little to do with one's actual death.

Death Is Not the Ending

We all believe we can't die because we simply have too much left to do. We have children to raise and goals to achieve and appointments in our PDA for next week. There is obviously a natural resistance to considering one's own death, but what I am saying is far more than "I don't want to face the fact that life will not last." The harder question by far is, "Does my life really have meaning?"

No matter how I try to escape the reality of death, I know I will die. But do I really know what meaning my life is meant to have? It turns out that Christians are the most difficult people to interact with regarding these questions. They know that heaven is ahead and that their life is significant. They are so sure of this that they seldom allow themselves to doubt or question the precise meaning of their own life. The result is an unexamined life.

Their assumption is simple: if I live a good life, love my kids, do my best at work, support the PTA and the church and my kids' sports, then my life will have been good. But is this a good ending as God views endings? It's not a bad ending, but it misses what any truly good ending requires—the ardor and the sacrifice, the passion and the blood.

We each are responsible for writing our story, including our ending. The difference between living well versus writing well is that writing requires me to face the fact that my first draft is a mess, needs significant editing, and requires much more honesty, depth, and passion. Yet for most people, living well means simply doing our best according to the standards of our culture. Am I really willing to move toward the kind of meaning that far exceeds being a "good" person? Am I ready to embrace the true meaning of my life and head to a wildly full ending?

The Meaning of a Good Ending

I have met a legion of people who are remarkable and glorious, but when asked if their life has mattered beyond their family and friends, they scoff at the thought. And when they are pressed further as to whether their life has been a glorious story moving toward a fantastic ending, the scoffing grows into wide-eyed, contemptuous incredulity. They have lived less in light of the story of God and more by the inevitabilities of life's demands. In other words, they allow circumstances to write their story. The Author is somehow absent from the process.

A good but unexamined life will be high on duty and not likely to celebrate the odd paradoxes, the ironic coincidences, and the humor of being dirt. Remember, we are clay. Adam wasn't named Red by accident.

So why don't we see our life as a great story and its ending as compelling and life-changing? My life is a play, a drama, and it will have a final line that sums up and completes all that has come before it. I write my own completion in the way I choose to spend my life.

We are called to coauthor the ending according to the themes that the primary Author has penned for us. We are called to take up our pen and follow him. It is the enormous humility of the sovereign Author to give us a voice in the dialogue. And not only does he want us to write, but he cheers us on. He writes, allows us to coauthor, and then is mesmerized by what we write with him. This amazing arrangement ought not to be, but it is. No wonder coauthoring takes faith.

The ending of my story is how I lived my life toward an aim, a finish that is worth both dying for and living for. If I live my life for me alone, then my story is as dull as my self-absorption, even if I have survived untold adventures. But if I live my life for Someone more important than myself and I have sacrificed, nobly risked, been humbled, learned, grown, and given, then my life is headed toward a glorious ending.

What makes my life a glorious bestseller is that my plot reveals not a mere moral or lesson but the very person and being of God. A merely good life reveals little beyond the fact that goodness exists. But a life that knows its plot, characters, setting, dialogue, and themes will possess a clear and abiding passion that reveals something unique about the Author. A life that is familiar with its story reveals much about the character of God.

I don't believe God is so concerned that we build ministries—or companies, families, or any other human legacy—to his glory. His glory is grown when we simply live out the calling he has given us. We give him much greater glory when we are aware of our calling, live intentionally, and live with passion. That's how we coauthor our own story.

But how in the world do we know our calling? I've seen that our calling always seems associated with the name that God gives each one of us. And how do we discover our name? We study the contours of our story and the embedded characters, tragedies, and plot to discover our name and calling. As we read our story, we learn what God has in store for our life and our ending.

To learn how to read our story, we must take responsibility to be the coauthor, with God, of our story. We must also learn to read what already has been written to know what needs to happen in the next chapter. We need to know what type of story we are in, its setting and characters, and our unique role or name in the narrative. Basically, my tale calls me to know what sort of name God has given me.

Telling Your Story

At the end of each chapter, you will find questions designed to help you think more specifically about your own story. These questions are taken from the companion to this book, *To Be Told Workbook*. (For more questions like these, and to take a guided journey in telling and writing your story, see *To Be Told Workbook*.)

Think about your life with this idea in mind: your life is made up of stories, each one possessing a beginning, a middle, and eventually an end. "Ending are meant to be a sensual, wild fullness of all that came before." How do you celebrate when there is a satisfying close to one of your stories?

chapter two

what's your real name?

Others Name Us, but Only God Knows Our Name

We dislike matter, that is ourselves, because we are
destined to matter, because anonymous matter is called
death. Perhaps it isn't matter we dislike, perhaps it's
anonymity. The anonymity to which we are destined—
the loss of name—is what we repress at any price.
HÉLÈNE CIXOUS

It was the biggest speaking event of my life. To this day I don't know why
I was invited to be part of Willow Creek's Leadership Conference. There
were seven thousand people in the audience where I was speaking and
thirty thousand more watching from various teleconference sites.

The night before the conference, when my wife and I arrived in Chicago, I was relaxed and confident. I would be talking about the intersection of character and leadership. It was not so much that I was confident about my own character and leadership skills. Just the opposite: I was exceedingly aware that I am a graduate-school president by default. No one else on our leadership team wanted the position. To apply for accreditation, we needed to fill in a name for president on the application form. My name was penciled in.

The source of my confidence in speaking on leadership was that I was going to talk about how leaders often mess up. I had messed up so frequently and so naturally that speaking on the topic would be a breeze. The outline was well established in my mind, and I went to bed early.

Then God awakened me at about one in the morning. How do I know it was God and not something I ate before retiring? I don't. But I heard an inner voice say, "Wake up." I sat bolt upright in bed only to hear the next words: "The outline for your talk sucks. Get up and change it." I have no idea if God actually uses the word *sucks,* but if he doesn't, then it was all in my subconscious.

No matter. Intuitively I knew my outline was lacking. Why I didn't realize this in the weeks before baffles me. But at that moment I knew. I turned on a light and took a seat at the hotel-room desk. *I am so tired, and now I'm terrified. What do you want me to do?* I got out a piece of paper and started writing. Within thirty minutes I had an outline that was simple and cogent. I went back to bed and slept like a baby.

But there is always the next morning. My wife, Becky, and I arrived at the conference site, where I had only a moment to consider what I was doing. I was sitting with Bill Hybels, senior pastor of Willow Creek Community Church, on my left and Becky on my right. It was a wild and glorious sensation. The music was incredible; the drama, spectacular. Bill introduced the morning's agenda, and I was more excited than ever to be there.

The last time I had checked the outline of my talk, I had pushed my glasses up on my head, intending, of course, to take them off and put them in my pocket. But before I could do so, I heard my name being spoken and felt the touch on my shoulder from a member of the production crew. I had no choice but to walk immediately to the podium.

What was I doing here? I looked at the thousands of faces in the audience and thought, *They know perfectly well that I have no right to be here.* You might think that's an exaggeration, but at that moment I didn't realize how true that sentiment was for many in the audience. One pastor told me nearly a year later that when he saw me shuffle to the podium, glasses on my head, my right pant leg stuck inside the top of my boot, he said to one of his companions, "I got the winner."

And he didn't mean that in a complimentary way.

Each year this group of friends picks the one conference speaker whom they suspect will be the least capable of the ten scheduled speakers. Though Willow Creek brings in the best of the best, each year there is one speaker whom some in the audience feel is not quite up to par. And each year the people in this small group place bets on the one they suspect will be the least capable.

I was this man's pick, and he felt confident he had chosen a winner. Or, in this case, the loser.

Apparently I disappointed him. My talk went well, and when I sat down, I was honored with a standing ovation. I was dumbstruck. Bill Hybels touched me on the arm and told me I had done an excellent job. His commendation was thrilling, but I needed to hear from the one person in the audience who truly mattered, my wife.

When I saw Becky's eyes, I was terrified. The sound of the applause was like thunder around me, but I saw in her face utter incredulity. She was stunned. At first I thought she was shocked by how well I had done. My words slipped out in an insecure slide: "Did I do okay?"

She leaned forward so I could hear: "I never knew you looked so Jewish." I heard each word, but I had no idea what she had just said. I asked her out loud, "What? What did you say?" She repeated, "I never knew you looked so Jewish. And, yes, you did a wonderful job."

I thought, *She's nuts.* What I didn't know was that God had intended that moment from the foundation of the earth. He had written my wife's story in such a way that she would speak those words right then at the prompting of the Spirit. In an odd way, Becky blessed me with her strange remark. At a moment when my name and my story felt alive, powerful, and blessed, she inadvertently reminded me that she doesn't fully know me. And if the person who knows me most on this earth doesn't fully recognize my face, do I? Do I know my name and my story? Do I know my father? In a moment of glory, Becky unnamed me and perhaps unwittingly invited me to listen more carefully to the name that will one day be mine—the name God will give me when my story on this earth ends.

THE POWER OF A NAME

Our name is our identity. The syllable(s) and sound of our name likely mean more to us than any other word or sound we'll ever hear. Dale Carnegie developed a multimillion-dollar business based on teaching people to win friends and influence people by saying someone's name a minimum of three times during a conversation. People apparently love to hear their own name. A famous television sitcom sold the setting and premise for the show with the line, "You want to go where everybody knows your name." Just like you, I want to be noticed, known, and enjoyed. We desire a powerful name.

In the ancient Near East a name conferred meaning and a future "to be lived up to or lived down."[1] A name marked a person with a set of expectations that determined the person's place in the family and in the world. Today it is rare that parents first study a child in order to give the child a name that fits. Far more often we pick a family name, or we choose a name that sounds good and has a meaning that we like. The Hebrew process of naming was exactly the opposite. A name was chosen that reflected the unique calling and character of the child.

It is for this reason that many Bible characters were renamed later in life. When Jacob's name was changed to Israel, he should have been thankful. Jacob means con artist, slime ball, card swindler, and used-car salesman. He was identified at birth as one who would hang on to his brother's heel and do all he could to manipulate the world to his advantage. After meeting God in a divine mugging, where he wrestled with God for his life and a blessing, God renamed him Israel, which means "one who struggles with God."[2] As this example illustrates, a name puts us in community, gives us our identity, and marks us for what may one day be our calling.

My name is Dan. The root meaning of the word is the notion of judging with wisdom. It also has a meaning of being crafty or snakelike. I didn't know that until recently, but decades ago a seminary friend gave me the name Nahash. The name is the Hebrew word for "snake." I was given the nickname Nahash because my wife worked at a restaurant that allowed her to take her uneaten lunch home with her. The next day I would dine on my wife's lunch, enjoying steak, fabulous Reuben sandwiches, or thick turkey and cranberry creations. My friend ate the typical graduate-student fare of cold cuts and peanut butter. At the time, he didn't know of my past run-ins with the law. He didn't realize how true a name he had given me, but knowing his discernment, I was not surprised the name Nahash spoke to him of who I was.

Between Two Names

Each change in name points to a day when we will receive an entirely new name. The Bible tells us that those who seek God will one day be given a new name: "Everyone who is victorious will eat of the manna that has been hidden away in heaven. And I will give to each one a white stone, and on the stone will be engraved a new name that no one knows except the one who receives it."[3] When I stand before God, I will be given a new name in a moment of tender, inconceivable intimacy. No one will speak that name but the Most High God. No one will whisper that name to me but my divine Lover. It is worth living our life well in the midst of the darkest heartache and greatest uncertainty just to hear that name spoken.

The passage also reminds us that we are living in a world in-between. We are between two names. We know our name; we don't know what our new name will be. The greatest tragedy of life is that most of us, including many of us who are deeply spiritual, forget that we don't yet know our true name. The result of forgetting is that we lose sight of the truth that we're on a journey to live out the story God has written for us and to thereby find his name for us.

Paradoxically, we're moving toward the discovery of something we don't yet know but have already received. Even without knowing the Bible or the notion of the already and the not yet, every one of us human beings experiences the tension between who we are and who we will one day become. To anticipate becoming a new person holds great hope as well as trepidation. This reality is too terrifying, too utterly alien and impossible to hold on to for long, so we forget and escape to the conventions of a good life. We set as our goal to be good, not to be named.

The word *mores,* the Latin word that means "convention," is where we get our word *morality.* We settle for the morality of our community in order to fit in, to not be too different, odd, or undesirable. And in that placid counterfeit of true life, we find respite from the questions that seek us out when we stare into the sky. In the norms of our world, we find a name that seems to fit us, but we intuitively know that the name our church, family, friends, and business associates speak to us is not the truest name that will be spoken. Or so we hope.

Listen to the testimony of an accomplished CEO who puts words to how easy it is to get lost in the corporate game and lose one's way. He was given a name, and it took him away from his unique path. "While I was driving home," he said, "it hit me: Honeywell was changing me more than I was changing Honeywell. I wasn't building anything; I wasn't creating anything. Sure, I was leading, but I no longer knew where my leading was leading to. I realized that I too was becoming imprisoned by the Game."[4]

This man was a corporate warrior whose life became what he wore and how he was received. He discarded his heart and wore a mask to fit into his company's culture. His success became his doom, and that truth hit him squarely in the face: "I've gained the world and lost my soul."

He left Honeywell and became the CEO of a smaller company. This move would not have occurred had he not been "hit" on the way home from work. Often when our world rips apart, we are able to see more easily what our story is and to hear more clearly what our name is.

Something must awaken us to the fact that we are asleep. And what awakens us is usually a moment of exposure when we see that the conventions that guide our steps and promise us a good life are nothing more than illusions. The stark reality that we have lived someone else's life and not our own whacks us on the side of the head. The journey of our story truly begins right then, when we start to see that the name we have been given is not our truest name.

Even when we are confident about the path we are to walk and the mission we are to live, a knowing ache compels us to keep our eyes open for more clues, for signs that whisper a name we can't yet hear. Our drama has to do with both how we lost our path and our name, and how we stumble forward to hear the voice of our Author and Namer. We often lose our path and our name due to the stories and names we acquire from our family of origin.

In the Name of the Father and Mother

At birth I was Dan Price, not Dan Allender. My father's name, Price, most likely was changed from the German Jewish name Preiss. The name Preiss likely sounded too Jewish for my relatives, who wished to blend in to their WASPish world with greater ease. I only had that name for four years, years that I don't recall except from the occasional stories I've heard from my mother. Seldom do any of us recall the actual events of our own first five years of life. Every now and then a few hazy images or scenes are unearthed, but at that age we don't think in narrative sequence, and therefore we can't recall those images as a story.

We simply remember what we are told or what the pictures from our photo albums tell us. The stories told are freeze frames, and they are family myths. They may be true, or they may be the preserved fictions that enable a family to mark how a son or daughter will fit into the family narrative.

A friend of mine was told from his earliest memory that he was born angry and depressed. He was the youngest in a family and had three older sisters. He was treasured by his sisters, and apparently he became the rope in a tug of war between his sisters and his mother. His mother was not fond of the girls, who were the delight of their father. The mom therefore marked her son with the epithet Problem in order to be the only one who could soothe him.

The name he was given—Angry and Depressed—marked him for most of his thirty-two years. He was the moody child. He was artistic and sensitive, and the only person said to be able to understand him was his mother. His relationship with his mother has been full of awkward intimacy, contempt, and need. He was named by his place in the family story. We all are.

Families are not always as damaging as this mother was when she named her son. Her act of violence was likely not conscious and evil but unwitting and defensive. She was acting out her story, which was set into motion by her mother and father, whose story was set into motion, of course, by their families.

Clearly each of us is a collage of stories. Most of those stories are lost to the telling, and the stories we know are seldom the stories that are most illuminating, since they often serve to hide or dull the far more revealing family stories full of heartache and shame. Every family has shame they wish to hide. In every family, there are unfaithful cousins, wine-bibbing aunts, eccentric uncles, lazy brothers, gossiping sisters, or not fully reputable fathers. At best, stories are told with the benevolence of laughter. If these stories are questioned, there is a genial hush or a condescending look among those who know that it is best to tell no more.

So we grow up in a sea of stories told in a way that fits what we want others to know about us. The stories told in most families are a kind of propaganda. The tragedy is that often these stories are simply a form of disinformation, as they were for my friend who was wrongly named Angry and Depressed. It took him three decades to see that this name was not true to the name he was given by God. But our families name us without knowing the consequences. So our life is a journey to discover our true name, though, sadly, many of us never choose to begin the search.

Most of us don't know where we are going or why because we're too busy to think about it. For the same reason, most of us have never considered the themes of our story or pondered the meaning of our name. Doing so appears a little too esoteric, too self-indulgent, or perhaps a pointless waste of time.

Studying our story is one of the most difficult tasks of life. How do we come to hear and name our own name? How do we come to read our own story and also write it? How do we gain a sense of who we are to become on the basis of what has already happened?

We are embedded in story, yet reading and interpreting story is our foremost means of finding out the meaning of life. Our story is made up of countless moments in our life in addition to the stories given to us from other sources. For the Christian the prime source is the Bible.

This idea that story is important might make sense to us on some theoretical level, but it seems impossible to look into our own story to study its trajectory. Part of the problem is that we don't want to take the risk. But the other aspect is that over time all our stories blend together in memory.

So before we study our stories, we need first to apprehend the needed background and context.

Toward that end, to study the story of our life, we must consider how stories are organized and constructed. To get our bearings, let's look at the tale that is already being told about my name—and yours.

Telling Your Story

Do you have an inkling of the name that God will one day give you? On dark nights of the soul, what do you fear your name will be? In the midst of buoyant hope, what do you wish your name might be?

chapter three

what makes a good story?

A Better Way to Read Your Tragedies

One of the clearest indications of a flawed life
story is its failure to give one the sense of purpose
and conviction necessary to live life with an
acceptable degree of optimism and resolve.
A failed story no longer encourages the kind
of life you feel it is important to live.
DANIEL TAYLOR

The best stories share certain features. You might not like the plot or the
ending, and you may despise some of the characters, but you still have to
admit that these stories are powerful and effective.

Think about a father from thousands of years ago who was bigger than life, a man whose name lives on in daily news reports of violence and turmoil in a strategic region of the world. A man who wrestled with God and lived to tell about it. A man who gave his twelve sons different names, who treated each one differently, and whose act of naming them had far-reaching consequences. The man is Jacob, later renamed Israel, and God wrote his story.

Now Jacob loved Joseph more than any of his other children
because Joseph had been born to him in his old age. So one day
he gave Joseph a special gift—a beautiful robe. But his brothers
hated Joseph because of their father's partiality. They couldn't say
a kind word to him.

One night Joseph had a dream and promptly reported the
details to his brothers, causing them to hate him even more....

When Joseph's brothers saw him coming, they recognized him
in the distance and made plans to kill him. "Here comes that
dreamer!" they exclaimed. "Come on, let's kill him and throw him
into a deep pit. We can tell our father that a wild animal has eaten
him. Then we'll see what becomes of all his dreams!"...

So when Joseph arrived, they pulled off his beautiful robe and
threw him into the pit. This pit was normally used to store water,
but it was empty at the time. Then, just as they were sitting down
to eat, they noticed a caravan of camels in the distance coming
toward them. It was a group of Ishmaelite traders taking spices,
balm, and myrrh from Gilead to Egypt.

Judah said to the others, "What can we gain by killing our
brother? That would just give us a guilty conscience. Let's sell

Joseph to those Ishmaelite traders. Let's not be responsible for his death; after all, he is our brother!" And his brothers agreed. So when the traders came by, his brothers pulled Joseph out of the pit and sold him for twenty pieces of silver, and the Ishmaelite traders took him along to Egypt.[1]

Your family and your world may be pretty "normal" and relatively happy, but most of the families portrayed in the Bible are not. Your life may not be littered with obvious tragedies, but the stories of the Bible are pockmarked by the foolishness, envy, and madness that make a story worth reading. Lives that are "normal" and predictable don't hold our attention. It is only when huge obstacles arise that a story becomes compelling. And the story of Joseph and his brothers is anything but a "normal" story.

When asked to describe a story, Hollywood screenwriter Robert McKee, whose students have written, directed, and produced notable films such as *Forrest Gump*, *Erin Brockovich*, and *The Color Purple*, said this:

> Essentially, a story expresses how and why life changes. It begins
> with a situation in which life is relatively in balance: you come to
> work day after day, week after week, and everything's fine. You
> expect it will go on that way. But then there's an event—in screen-
> writing, we call it the "inciting incident"—that throws life out of
> balance. You get a new job, or the boss dies of a heart attack, or a
> big customer threatens to leave. The story goes on to describe how,
> in an effort to restore balance, the protagonist's subjective expecta-
> tions crash into an uncooperative objective reality. A good storyteller
> describes what it's like to deal with these opposing forces, calling
> on the protagonist to dig deeper, work with scarce resources, make

nothing of shalom

difficult decisions, take action despite risks, and ultimately discover the truth. All great storytellers since the dawn of time—from the ancient Greeks through Shakespeare and up to the present day— have dealt with this fundamental conflict between subjective expectation and cruel reality.[2]

Good stories tell about the intersection of desire ("subjective expectation") and tragedy ("cruel reality"). A story begins when our desires collide head-on with reality. Sometimes reality is impersonal, like a storm that sets into motion a flash flood that kills nine kids on a bus going to Bible camp. But other times the cruelty is volitional. It could involve envious brothers, an unwise father who favors one son over the others, and a talkative, gifted younger brother who shares more about his dreams and desires than he should. Good stories demand tragedy, an "inciting incident." And inciting incidents will always intensify our desire to listen to what the story is telling us—unless the inciting incident happens in our own story. Often, when it occurs in our life, we want the story to be resolved and the problem solved—and quickly! We love stories as long as they happen to someone else.

Stories don't give answers, but they do offer perspective. They provide a window through which we can look for patterns of life. Peering through the window then leads to more compelling stories and finally deeper wisdom. Wisdom ultimately isn't a formula or a conclusion but a way of being in the world that leads to a more truthful and more beautiful good. Stories lure us because we sense this good hidden within them.

We hear or read a story with a sense of where it is taking us, knowing that at some point something is going to happen that defies our expectations. Then we wait to see where the story will take us next. As each new surprise or confirmation shows itself, we add up clues and rework our hypotheses about where the story is going. In this way we are never passive recipients of a story: as we read, we anticipate how the plot will progress, which is a form of writing along with the author. It is no different with our own story.

After all, stories tend to follow a common structure that takes us on a journey. If we pay attention to how the author builds the structure, we will get a sense of the kind of story being told and the meaning that we are to encounter. Just as the Bible moves from Creation to the Fall through millenniums of redemption to an ending, so all stories move from shalom to a shattering and then to a search that comes to a temporary but satisfying ending. Each portion of a story has a particular style and content that tells the story within the story.

SHALOM

Stories begin with life at peace. Such shalom is not merely an absence of tension or the presence of perfect pleasure. It is a deep inner and external harmony when disparate parts flow together in a unity that is greater than the sum of the parts. It is like an excellent choir. At the state competition, when the tension and desire to do well are at their height, each member digs deeper and sings with an abandon that in turn stirs the combined whole, including the conductor, to reach even higher. As the piece moves to completion, the harmony intensifies to a level that is beyond what the choir has ever reached before. It is an experience of the fullness and beauty of shalom.

Shalom often comes in a moment of tranquillity and innocence. As I wrote the last paragraph, I watched an eight-month-old child stand in her mother's lap and peer into her mother's eyes. Her hands caressed her mother's cheeks, and as she cooed, her mother echoed her tones. I stopped writing and stared. The moment of innocent, tender play between mother and daughter was captivating. Such shalom is simultaneously invigorating and restful. It stirs and calms. It can bring the heart to a rest that may lead to sleep, but it is more likely to draw us to awe and wonder.

We all have moments of shalom. It is the moment we sat on our grandmother's lap and played with her pearl necklace. It is going downstairs on a winter morning and warming our feet against the furnace vent. I recall seeing my pajama pants billow with the flowing heat that made my toes toasty. I remember putting my head on a pillow to read a picture book until my mom called me to a breakfast of pancakes and warm syrup. That was shalom.

At first in the story about Joseph, we sense an idyllic life. Joseph was the favored son of Jacob, an old man who had suffered untold struggle due in large part to his own scheming and manipulation of others. Jacob was blessed with this beautiful son toward the end of his days, and he honored Joseph with a prized multicolored coat. The significance of the coat's colors is simple: Joseph was his father's favorite. He knew it, and he enjoyed the power of his position. The result was a vocal and commanding presence with his older brothers. He felt free to violate the custom of deference to one's elders. Joseph was the inciting incident in the lives of his older brothers. He disturbed their shalom.

A moment of shalom is a taste of life in Eden. It is life without sin, tragedy, emptiness, or fear. Search your own memory for moments of shalom. Recall moments of rest, safety, and warmth. Those moments are likely associated with a person and a place and a season in our life, usually prior to beginning school or in our early elementary years. For many of us, recalling those moments produces not nostalgia and pleasure but significant sadness. Those times are gone, and often they were lost when shalom was shattered. But it is crucial that we remember those moments when our story was at peace and we felt the warm and kind wind that blew from Eden into our life.

To remember is to anticipate with groaning the future day when our past shalom will appear in glory at the Day of the Lord. Our willingness to hold dear the moments of past shalom prepares us to imagine a new and better day and, even more, to move toward that day with passion and purpose.

Shalom Shattered

Shalom is shattered by sin, by the intrusion of a lie, a distortion of the truth that mars the pleasure of being naked, transparent, trusting, and true. Shalom is not shattered merely by the presence of something "not good" because, in the Garden of Eden, God said that it was "not good" for man to be alone. Apparently, God wanted Adam to know loneliness and absence in order to enter the glory of presence and companionship. Mere absence is not tragedy, nor is our shalom shattered when we experience loneliness. Instead, shattering occurs when our dignity is assaulted and death enters to divide and destroy.

Consider the so-called innocent teasing of childhood. A group of kids gathers around a timid classmate who is overweight: "Fatty pants, fatty pants, you're a big blubber butt!" Such words attack the most tender and raw part of the child's being. Such words shatter shalom as sin severs trust and grows shame like a cancer. The result of the shattering is death. In every story, in every life, there are moments of death that take away our name and rename us as strangers, orphans, or widows.

At the moment of being unnamed, we are thrown into our story. We lose the name Friend and are given the name Reject. Our story prior to the point of being unnamed is a mild fluctuation between good and evil. It may be a boring or rather empty story, but at least it's safe. Then tragedy enters the garden, and we are forever changed as we are cast from the sweet protection of shalom. From that point we embark on a journey that offers only intermittent moments of rest. Our life is anything but mild, anything but safe.

Joseph's life followed this pattern. He was relatively happy until he went to find his brothers. Apparently, he wasn't used to being out in the rough-and-tumble world, but for some reason he was allowed to travel. His short trip became the starting point of a long and agonizing journey to an inhospitable foreign land.

Obviously shalom had been shattered long before this event, because Joseph's brothers already hated him. But once the opportunity arose for them to punish him, Joseph's life journey truly began. Tragedy always moves our story forward in a way that shalom could never accomplish.

Joseph's encounter with tragedy removed him from his father's benevolent provision. He went from Most Likely to Succeed into shackled slavery. Such a reversal of fortune, the shattering of shalom, takes away our identity, reverses our expectations, and steals from us the security of our name. No longer was Joseph Favored Son. He was now Powerless Slave.

Listen to your own memory of times when you were unnamed or destabilized by a shattering experience. Some moments are monstrous, such as death-dealing incidents of sexual abuse. Or these moments can be as subtle and common as being mocked on a playground. In either case, the shattering moves us from a place of shalom to a place that is harsh and unrelenting. The shattering brings us a keen awareness that we are alone and in danger. We are on our own.

44

This is a pivotal point of our story. We need to name those moments and identify their settings, characters, dialogue, and impact. Doing this requires enormous honesty and courage, but it moves us more deeply into the plot of our life where we can once again imagine and pursue shalom.

Shalom Sought

Once we are evicted from the shalom of Eden, we must figure out how to get food, where we are going to sleep, and how we will make our way in the world. It's inconceivable to consider what Adam and Eve felt during their first night east of Eden. Life in the wild, surrounded by the formidable darkness, would require a radical new choice: *Will I trust in God's goodness to protect me and provide for my needs, or will I trust in myself?*

The search for shalom is infused with the fundamental question of meaning: Is life as random, pointless, and absurd as it seems? Or is it ordained, purposeful, and meaningful? What will win—the abundant indications of randomness or our desire for more than we can see? The fact that we tell stories that are given meaning by structure implies an awareness that life is not essentially random. Life surely has meaning, no matter how obscure or confusing.

The search for that meaning is given structure by honesty, desire, and risk.

Honesty Is Naming That We Are No Longer in Eden
Our shalom has been compromised; we've been cast out of Eden. But an amazing number of us never begin this journey because we won't fully admit that we have been exiled, orphaned, and widowed. We want to believe we are still citizens and heirs, not aliens and fatherless children. But

the story we are to live and write doesn't truly begin until we face what we have lost and then turn to see the horizon of uncertainty ahead. Our story will gain momentum and depth only to the degree that we honestly embrace both loss and fear.

Desire Bridges Our Past and Our Future

Desire takes form through our dreams. For Joseph, dreaming literally plunged him into his plight. Telling his brothers that he saw them bowing down to him in a dream fueled their conspiracy to sell him into slavery.

But later, Joseph's dreaming reversed the shattering of his shalom. He was called from prison to report to Pharaoh what God had been telling him about Egypt's future in a dream. We're in the presence of a good story when the flaw that shatters shalom is also the doorway to redemption. That is, Joseph's being exiled (the shattering) led to his relationship with Pharaoh (his redemption). Whether it be our own flaw or the sin of others, God uses the raw material of sin to create the edifice of his redeemed glory.

This point cannot be overemphasized: your plight is also your redemption. The Bible assumes that its stories are also our story. Abraham, the father of faith, is sent off into exile. He's a settled man with a comfortable life, but God makes him an alien in a foreign land. Like Abraham, we will be called by God to leave our place of comfort. Isaac, the son of laughter, is redeemed from death by God's provision, and we will know God's provision as well. Jacob, the son of Isaac, takes redemption into his own hands and ends up being an alien like his grandfather.

We are Abraham, Isaac, and Jacob. Their stories are a paradigm of our own. Each of us is called, redeemed, and exiled—again and again. Along the way, we are called to make choices consistent with the character we are called to play. Our story evolves as we face the tough decisions that come our way.

Joseph was forced to make a series of agonizing choices. He was a slave serving in a position of trust when Potiphar's wife invited him into her bedchamber. He could choose to have illicit sex with the wife of one of the most powerful men in Egypt. But instead of choosing pleasure, he fled her grasp. This was the right choice, of course, but Joseph's integrity got him into trouble. Potiphar's wife accused him of rape, and he was sent to jail. No matter that the accusation was false. Joseph went to prison nonetheless.

And Joseph's story increases in intensity. Earlier in his life his pride had caused him to be dumped into the pit; later his integrity got him into deeper trouble.

In Joseph's story, the Storyteller is telling us something about life and about our own story. He is showing us that life is not predictable. The simple equation "Do good and good will come to you, but do bad and you will pay the price" doesn't hold. It is more accurate to say, "Do good or do bad, but in either case disaster awaits." The search for shalom, for example, took Joseph to prison where he was face to face with two men whose fates couldn't be more different from each other's. Joseph again told the truth boldly. And just at the point when you think his agony was finally over, it began again. Instead of being rescued from prison, Joseph was left in chains. Two long years passed before one of Joseph's former cellmates—the one whose dream had been interpreted favorably—remembered Joseph and mentioned to Pharaoh his ability to interpret dreams.

Joseph no doubt lamented his situation, but God is not bound by time, nor is our story. We desperately want our situation solved. We want resolution. But God unfolds the plot in his own time. It is in our months or years of waiting that our story comes to maturity. It is over a lifetime of stories that he turns our desire toward him.

Desire lies at the heart of who God made us to be, who we are at our core. Desire is both our greatest frailty and the mark of our highest beauty. Our desire completes us as we become one with our Lover, and it separates us from him and brings death as it wars against his will. Desire is life and it is death.

Desire is also at the core of an honest story, and it is the core tension of all life. If we choose to read our story, then we are choosing to enter a wild-and-woolly process of writing and editing our life to embrace both loss and fear, dreams dashed as well as dreams enlivened by resurrected desire.

Risk Requires Bleeding for Our Dreams

A dream without suffering is little more than a fantasy. Risk, the third element that gives structure to our search, involves bleeding. Too many people are missing their story because they're watching the stories of others. We live story vicariously through television, sports, magazines, and talk shows. Such stories may occasionally educate us, but most often they sedate us. They free us from admitting that our own life is dull and lifeless. They attract us because they offer life without risk. They are deathly safe.

Fantasy often involves legitimate desire. It is not wrong to ponder what I'd do if a car veered off the road in front of me or what I might do with a million dollars inherited from a long-lost uncle. Such daydreams are highly revelatory, but what they lack is blood. Fantasy becomes a life dream when I'm willing to plunge into the cold water of reality. I don't need to inherit a million dollars before I can give away money, nor do I need that much money before I can embrace the passions and pleasures that are woven into the fabric of my life. Such action—such living—only takes a willingness to bleed.

So listen to the converging stories of the present. There is most likely just a handful of stories standing front and center in your life. They involve either loss and uncertainty or great opportunity and risk. Whether the story takes place in the arena of business, family, friendships, enemies, love, service, or play, you can be assured that the inciting events call for you to sacrifice your comfort and ease in order for your story to move forward. It's easy to ignore such inciting events. Just turn on the television or crack open a trashy novel. It's easy to flee your story.

But if we honestly name the passionate desires of our heart, and if we risk seeing those desires come to be, the plot of our life story will begin to move with greater intentionality. Yet the only way we can keep walking on that path is to allow ourself moments to rest and celebrate the temporary climax of a story in a denouement.

DENOUEMENT

A denouement is not a complete or fully resolved ending but a satisfying closure to a story. It means in French "an untying, a relaxing of a knot of complexity." Denouement is the rest that comes when all the disparate plot lines of a story, gnarled and taut, have been untied and an order has come about that brings a new moment of shalom.

The story of Joseph's brothers' going to Egypt to buy grain intensified the story of Joseph's rise to power. At that time he was second in command to Pharaoh, but his rise in status did not signal the story's denouement. In fact, the story became even more complex. Joseph trapped his brothers as they once trapped him. He gave instructions to them without revealing his identity, and a series of events unfolded in which first, Simeon had to remain with him until Benjamin (the youngest) was brought back to Joseph, and second, after Joseph framed Benjamin for theft, Judah had to plead to be taken as a slave in place of the youngest. The brothers' terror during these events revealed an honest and good grief, and eventually it melted Joseph's heart. He couldn't hide his identity any longer, and there was a reunion with his brothers, a partial denouement. But then came the ultimate denouement to this story that is beautiful in its multilevel complexity: the tension fully unraveled when the brothers returned with their father, Jacob, and the reunited family wept and rejoiced together. Not only were the separated brought back together, but the brothers' earlier deception actually served as the basis of the family's redemption.

Tragedy mars shalom, but denouement invites us to remember our innocence and dream of a day of even greater redemption. Denouement is an ending that serves as the prelude for a new beginning; there is always the next turn in the road. A new story begins the moment the old one ends. But a denouement is a respite that calls us to stop the journey for a brief interlude—to eat, drink, sing, dance, and tell our story to others.

All good endings call us to ponder our ultimate end. A good ending, like a good wedding or funeral, calls us to take it all in and meditate. The word *meditate* in Greek means to chew something over like a cow chews its cud. A good ending calls us to ponder in the midst of pleasure.

We must let the juices of a good ending sweeten the morsel of a story. Endings are not merely times for reflection; they are also seasons for celebration. We are to dance in the arms of a good ending. One of our greatest failures in our busy, driven culture is that we don't celebrate the temporary untying of a complex narrative. We are too busy to take a break, so we settle in front of a television screen to see other people enter a denouement after their twenty-six minutes of "complexity."

What is your style of celebrating an ending? Do you only throw large parties after someone graduates, gets married, or dies? If so, then all the other endings in your story are lost in the wake of another day's busyness. Perhaps one of the reasons you and I don't party well is that we don't know what to do with the tragedies that linger in our life. Nor do we know what to do with the moments that shattered us, even as we look back after the damage has been richly, though not completely, resolved. When do we celebrate a denouement related to the struggle of being overweight, unwanted, angry, lonely, fearful, or ashamed? We don't. Can you imagine receiving an invitation to a party: "Join me in celebration of no longer believing I am stupid"? Or how would you go about inviting friends to join you to celebrate the richness of having encountered a huge moment of crisis and choosing not to withdraw or blame yourself but instead to tackle it and enjoy a great outcome?

We don't allow endings to be noted, let alone celebrated. Therefore we never allow denouement to invigorate the upward movement of a new story. And we will only love our story to the degree that we see the glory that seeps through our most significant shattering. To see that glory, we must enter into and read our tragedies with confidence that they will end better than we could ever imagine.

If we enter our story's heartache, we will hear the whisper of the name that will one day be ours. Because we live in a fallen world, we will encounter abandonment, betrayal, and shame. These experiences are inevitable, but they also provide the context necessary for coming to grips with how we will live our lives. In the midst of affliction, we become either our truest or our most false self.

In those moments of unnaming, when we have lost ourselves, we must remember to return to our past redemptions to find God's marks of glory on our abandonment, betrayal, and shame. We wrongly believe that we will be happy if we can escape the past. But without our past we are hollow and plastic beings who have only common names and conventional stories. When we enter into our story at the point we lost our name, we are most likely to hear the whisper of our new name. Remember, God is still writing.

YOUR STORY UNFOLDS

What we have accomplished so far in this book is seeing that every life is a story with a unique meaning, about a person who bears a unique name, and which shares a common structure with every other story. According to this structure, we all will journey through countless moments of shalom, shattering, and searching that bring us to a sweet season of rest and celebration. We don't just have stories; we *are* a story. It is our responsibility to know our story so we can live it out more intentionally and boldly for the Great Story, the gospel. God writes our story not just for our own enlightenment and insight, but to enlighten others and to reveal his own story through our story.

We are to read our past to gain a greater sense of how to write our life in the present. The more we take responsibility to write our present to honor the past, the greater the number of stories there will be in the future that are lived for his glory. For that reason, the remaining chapters of this book are about reading, writing, and arithmetic.

Reading Your Story

You might want to rush out and make a decision about a current life crisis, or you might want more clarity about what you are to do with your life. Whatever your situation, the mistake is to make a move without first reading your past—an exercise that is time-consuming and not immediately profitable. Reading your life is like reading any story: it takes patience and hope to keep turning one page after another. The next three chapters invite you to read and reflect on your story. You will begin to ponder your life's passions, tragedies, and character. The result ought to be a clearer sense of how God has already written your life. He was writing in the past, and what he wrote holds great meaning for your present and your future.

Writing Your Story

God has written our life, but he also calls us to coauthor it with him. We are not robots, passively living out a foreordained script. Instead we are coauthors with God, living out our part in God's larger story. And we know his path for our future when we look at our past. Our Author tells us what to do and where to go as we begin to coauthor our present and our future with him.

We are called by God to write a meaningful story that reveals an even greater story—his story, the Greatest Story. To do so, we must know the unique who, what, where, when, and how of living out redemption. Chapters 7 and 8 invite you to join God in writing your story.

The Arithmetic of Your Story

Reading, writing, and arithmetic—or more accurately, *multiplication*—summarize our highest calling. We read and write our stories for the sake of others and for God's glory. Our stories are not our own. Our stories are not to be read and written merely for our own benefit. My story is your story, and all our stories are for God. Therefore, I am to read, write, edit, tell, and celebrate your story as much as my own. That is the multiplication of story.

The final section of this book explores how prayer, fasting, and giving create a story feast that gives us all a taste of the coming banquet that ends this era of stories and begins a whole new universe of storytelling and story writing. When we multiply our stories, we come to love our own story as well as the stories of our family, friends, and enemies.

Let's start this process by reading.

Telling Your Story

As you think about your life, revisit scenes where you saw redemption and where it was absent; where great suffering occurred and where nondramatic, routine suffering occurred; where there was peace and where there was resolution. As you do this, you are recalling stories of shalom, shalom shattered, shalom sought, and denouement.

reading your story

chapter four

listening to what moves you

The Passion That Defines You

I think we ought to only read the kind of books that wound and stab us. If the book we are reading doesn't wake us up with a blow on the head, what are we reading it for? So that it will make us happy, as you write?… We would be happy precisely if we had no books, and the kind of books that make us happy are the kind we could write ourselves if we had to. But we need the books that affect us like a disaster, that grieve us deeply, like the death of someone we loved more than ourselves, like being banished into forests far from everyone, like a suicide. A book must be the axe for the frozen sea inside us.

FRANZ KAFKA, *Letters to Friends, Family, and Editors*

We are what we choose. And we choose whatever our deepest passion compels us to be and to do. To understand the truth of this simple principle, we must examine choice's power to shape our character.

A single choice can set the direction of our life. Countless movies and books explore the irrevocable impact of a single choice by imagining what would happen to others if we didn't exist or if someone traveled into the past to change one choice. It is impossible to foresee the avalanche of consequences that would follow.

Yet questions still arise when we consider the choices we make: Is our life determined for us, or is it written with our cooperation? Do we speak to our own condition and therefore write our future, or are we the elemental cogs in a vast epic of mechanical predestination?

We often feel both free and bound. People who like to think they are self-made know that much happened that was outside their control. At the same time, we often feel that we made a decision that had a determinative role in how our story played out. We know we are small, yet our choices have significant consequences for others. We intuit that we are both part of a larger story that is infinitely beyond us, untouched by our choice and design, yet also intimately and profoundly connected to a story that is personal and possibly far more profound and far-reaching than we can imagine. We live in the middle of both realities. We are both powerless and unimaginably powerful simply because we have the ability to choose.

I recall the day my life changed in ways I still do not fully comprehend. It came with a phone call at seven thirty in the morning a few days before spring term ended my first year in seminary. Someone shouted for me to come to the phone. I staggered out of bed and down the hall and muttered an incoherent "Yeah" into the receiver. The voice on the other end said, "This is David Nicholas." I said, "Who?" He replied, "I am the pastor at

Spanish River Presbyterian Church in Boca Raton, Florida." I had no idea who he was or what he wanted.

His voice boomed. "Look. Do you want a job this summer or not?" I flinched, straining my mind. Suddenly his name surfaced as I remembered a conversation with a friend of mine who attended a church in Florida. Without fully meaning to, I said yes to David Nicholas's offer of a job. He said, "Good. Be here in a week." I laughed and asked where Boca Raton was, and he said, "Buy a map."

How could this happen?

It happened and a story explains how. I had taken in a "homeless" seminary student named Tom, whose wife had been too ill to travel to school at the beginning of the term. I offered Tom a place in my room, and he stayed with me until his wife arrived a few weeks later. We ate lunch together often and developed a friendship. Toward the end of our first year, I decided to go to Europe to hang out and practice my German. Tom said it would be wise for me to work in a church instead. I found his suggestion hilarious. I told Tom that no church would take me, and he said his pastor was odd enough to take someone like me. I thought nothing about that conversation until the moment I was awakened to answer the telephone.

It was that church and that pastor who invited me to the glory of the ministry. It was that church that took me in, introduced me to Larry Crabb, counseling, preaching, and teaching, and opened my heart to the possibility that my life might actually be useful to God. One phone call— one yes that escaped from my mouth—changed the direction of my life.

We are the sum of every yes that we utter. I can look back over my life and see a series of yeses that took me to my wife, my calling, and my current labor. But it's rare that we see where a yes will take us at the moment we utter it. When I agreed to go to Boca Raton, it seemed strange and adventurous, but I had no idea it would be the one yes that would radically alter my life. Seldom do we know the implications of our choices.

Most of what we do day to day seems mundane, isolated, and lost in the sea of sameness. But underlying everything we choose is desire. It is desire that shapes when and to what we say yes. Why would I choose to say yes to an unknown place in Florida because a friend I met at seminary suggested I do so? It's because I listened to my heart. I was restless enough to head off to Germany with no real purpose, and I was just beginning to see that the gospel is true. My heart wanted something new and bold, and the phone call came right on cue.

Listen to Your Heart

We often refer to the core of our being as the heart. Our heart is more than our mind, deeper than our will, and truer than our emotions. It is the sum of our being. But even that doesn't accurately measure the totality of our being. There is something in every human being that is beyond our wildest comprehension in its capacity for both good and evil. I can do the utterly unexpected because the presence of eternity beats within me. In a phrase that causes my heart to swerve in wonder, the author of Ecclesiastes tells us that God "planted eternity in the human heart."[1] This isn't just pretty imagery. Eternity—a longing for God—fuels our passion. It guides our choices. It sets a course for our life.

Eternity pulses through my blood, and its course will never allow me fully to forget that I will one day stand face to face with a holy, just, and righteous God. I may largely ignore the vortex I am moving toward, but the law of love—the call to give oneself fully and completely to another—cries out in each cell of my being. So, in light of the pulse of eternity, how do I wish to live? We are all poised to become more of who we are and who we have not yet become.

A yes or a no reflects what we value most and determines the end toward which we will move. All decisions are guided by our projection of ourselves into the future, called our *ideal self.* We each see ourselves as being a certain kind of person with a specific set of values, beliefs, and dreams. In practice, however, we often are not what we want to be but instead end up choosing what others expect us to be. This is called our *ought self.* Avoid it. None of us will ever reach the ideal, but we can escape the ought in order to become what's called a *real self.* The real self is the one that lives honestly and ably in the middle between the ideal and the ought.

YOUR IDEAL SELF

I am an aging man who carries more weight and less hair than I did a year ago. But when I look in a mirror, I am usually surprised to see who is look-ing back at me. I still believe myself to be around twenty-eight, thin, with a full head of hair, taut skin, and a happy twinkle in my eye. What I've just described is my ideal body image. All of us have ideals for ourselves in such diverse and countless areas as worker, lover, fighter, financier, friend, spouse, parent, child, citizen, and believer. In each area we have an image that serves as a North Star to guide us to our potential. And each image has its roots in desire, dreams, memory, and people.

Furthermore, we are a complex of choices based on who we want to become. My son, for instance, dreams of being a great lacrosse goalie. He mimics his heroes and spends much of his day in activities designed to help him realize his dreams. He wanted to play football, but I forbade him to do so. I had played for nine years and had achieved success along with significant permanent injuries, and I didn't want my son to play a dangerous contact sport. He chose lacrosse, and though it has high contact, it is not a constant battering of one body against another.

The first day of practice, I dropped Andrew off at school with these parting words: "I don't care what you play, but whatever you do, *don't* pick goalie." Before the first game, the coach said he needed a volunteer to play goalie, and my son stepped forward. I watched as Andrew fielded hard balls thrown at more than sixty miles per hour. I was horrified. He was happy.

His choice was not entirely built on thwarting his father's will, but to a degree his decision was a way of saying, "You can limit my choices, but I won't always do what you want." So the path to becoming what we dream as ideal involves a series of risks, compromises, fights, and failures. The deepest passion fuels our ideal.

Passion is what makes us feel most alive. For one person it is reading Flannery O'Connor, and for another it is watching one's stock portfolio grow. It is not wrong to love literature or to want to make money on investments or to have a passion for both. Our ideal image of ourself is inextricably tied to our deepest passion. We will not know our true self unless we can name the passions that are tied to our ideal self.

Our ideal self is revealed in what we value (passion), how we understand the world (belief), and what we do to reach our ideal (behavior). Our passion, belief, and behavior fit together so intimately that I can say this with confidence:

- What we do is what we really value.
- What we value enough to do tells others what we really believe.
- What we really believe shapes what we will become.

My own failures in trying to lose weight serve as an apt illustration. I want to lose weight, but I've failed at it for more than a decade. I have lost and regained my excess weight enough times to have made at least five new people. I've failed to achieve my ideal body image. Why? Because I value something more deeply than I do my ideal body image. I value the image of a man who is satisfied, full, and at rest. I am more passionate about having a full stomach than I am about being thin. The proof of that is, of course, my behavior.

My passion—eating good food and being full—is fortified by the belief that I can't control my life or my suffering, but when I eat, I feel good. And I value feeling good more than looking good or being healthy. Therefore, dieting works well until something in life discourages me. Then I discard the diet and start eating.

So we always choose what we value most, even when our choice does us harm. We won't change our behavior until we first recognize what we value most deeply and then honestly face how our passions reinforce what we really believe. We can change our beliefs, but doing so won't alter our behavior until our beliefs transform our values. We can change what we do, but the changes won't last if our values and convictions are not transformed.

Each of us can begin the process of transformation by wrestling with these questions:

- What moves me most deeply?
- What do I most enjoy doing?
- Where do I find the greatest pleasure and joy?
- What is it about this activity, idea, or person that brings me such a sense of life?

Our passion moves us to choose one path over another, and it is as unique as a fingerprint. Our passion may be to cheat death by taking huge physical risks, or it may be to avoid suffering by choosing to avoid dangerous people, situations, and ideas. In either case we have an ideal that we are constantly measuring ourselves by, and how we measure up results in either disappointment or joy.

Our sense of who we most deeply want to be also runs headfirst into what others think we should be.

YOUR OUGHT SELF

Our ideals often get suffocated by the expectations of others. To continue the illustration, I may have an ideal body image that I never achieve because I don't want to suffer or I have no time to exercise. And the reason I don't have time to work out may be as simple as I'm too busy doing what others think I should do. And who are these infamous "others"? They are those who have helped form my character through the various roles I play.

The word *character* originally referred to a stylus or a tool that makes a groove in a piece of wood. A character came to mean whatever is marked or cut by a stylus, the pattern that an artist has carved into the raw material. Likewise, initially we are marked by the most dominant and influential people in our life. However, their marking can't fully form us without our participation. In fact, we adopt others' expectations of us by making them our own.

Ultimately, though, our role is cut by God. Our parents may have a huge hand in shaping our character as we either conform to or defy their desire. However, God orchestrates all of the influences in our life to blend a symphony of themes that reflects his purposes.

The role we choose is written by God but acted out by us. In this role we have the privilege of coauthoring the script and ad-libbing on stage. Yet God, by his creative force, imbues this role with its parameters and possibilities. He chose our era, our place of origin and our family, the shape of our bodies, our level of intelligence, and the stories that preceded us. We are not bound by what is given, nor are we free to ignore it. Our role emerges from what we experienced in our first stage—the family.

Our initial role in life arises in the matrix of what is required and what is possible. We fall into a family in a certain birth order, which sets up standard options. (A first child will be more responsible and ambitious than the second. The second will be sneakier, more watchful, and less pressured than the first.) We each develop sensitivity to our unique set of passions. (One child will know that she bears the responsibility to succeed. Another will know that his role is to bring laughter and joy, while a third will be responsible for taking away the family's shame and failure by being the scapegoat.)

It is difficult and often unnecessary to renounce the role that we play early in life. In fact, the role we are shaped to play is one, after profound redemption and revolution, we are meant to live out in the future. We should not hate and eschew the training we gain on the stage of family. Instead, we should explore it, because it is our earliest clue to our future name and calling.

So we live out a role, or we live according to a set of expectations of who we are and how we will engage with others. The role we play is both given and found. I had the role of being the translator or the messenger between my mother and father. My father was a profoundly uncommunicative man. He would often say to me, "Go calm your mom down. She's upset with something I've done, and she needs to talk." It was my job to provide her with "perspective" after she described the quarrel they'd just had. Here was the problem: The perspective I offered might get Dad off the hook, but it would make my mom feel guilty and unloved. On the other hand, if I chose to side with my mom, then I had to convince my dad of the legitimacy of her hurt.

It was a no-win world, so I found solace in books and, even more, in the staggering power and glory of words. In words I found a yes. In fact it was a divine yes that brought comfort and offered the hope of transformation. In the midst of words, I found my deepest sense of pleasure and passion. Where we find our passion—and the things that stoke that passion—will eventually become part of our character.

But what might your role be if you were the child of an opinionated and contemptuous parent? Instead of a translator, you might become an accommodating listener who serves as the amen corner, simply parroting the views of that dangerous parent. What might an accommodating listener become over many years? One woman who had been deeply intimidated by her angry mother became a gentle and kind presence for others. She knew the pain of being small, and her stance toward others was to enhance them whenever she could. The problem was that she was often too frightened to tell others the truth; therefore she was limited in her ability to give love.

Our role in our family of origin was given to us more than it was chosen by us. But we honed and perfected it as a means to save our families and in turn preserve ourselves. The role we are given is often predictable and well defined, but we seldom act it out in a mechanical fashion. Instead we customize the role to our way of being.

So which is it that really moves us—the ideal self or the ought self? The answer is obvious: we live in a state of constant compromise between the two. We sacrifice what is ideal for what is required, and vice versa. Most of the time it is nearly impossible to discern which self most deeply moves us.

Am I losing weight because it is healthy or because I will feel better about myself according to some general notion that defines an attractive male form? We're not free to do entirely what we want, because we're all people under obligation. The person who thinks of no one else is a narcissist. On the other hand, if I live with nothing but ought, then I am only what others have required of me. I'm a soulless sycophant.

What moves me should be the passions that God has written into my story, even if I don't fully understand what they are or why they exist. I must find them so I can become real.

Your Real Self

If you want to find wisdom about life, it's often best to read some of the great writing found in children's stories. Exactly what does it mean to be real? Margery Williams tells us in *The Velveteen Rabbit:*

> "What is REAL?" asked the Rabbit one day. "Does it mean having things that buzz inside you and a stick-out handle?"
>
> "Real isn't how you are made," said the Skin Horse. "It's a thing that happens to you. When a child loves you for a long, long time, not just to play with, but REALLY loves you, then you become Real."
>
> "Does it hurt?"
>
> "Sometimes." For he was always truthful. "When you are Real, you don't mind being hurt."
>
> "Does it happen all at once, like being wound up, or bit by bit?"
>
> "It doesn't happen all at once. You become. It takes a long time. That's why it doesn't often happen to people who break easily, or who have sharp edges, or who have to be carefully kept. Generally,

by the time you are Real, most of your hair has been loved off, and your eyes drop out, and you get loose in the joints and very shabby. But those things don't matter at all, because once you are Real you can't be ugly, except to people who don't understand."[2]

So what really moves us? In light of that passage, it's whatever we love. If I love the feeling of being full, satisfied, and content, I will love the ease that any false god like food can provide. Why am I more motivated by the soothing satisfaction of a doughnut than I am by the thrill of working out at the gym? The answer, in part, is because doughnuts require less risk, suffering, and loss than a thirty-minute workout. And I love what takes away pain and suffering more than I love what is true, good, or lovely.

I'm called to be real. I am real if I have been loved and if I know love to be better than sorrow, stronger than death, truer than any spin. Real is not an ideal because I'm real only after all my parts have been worn off. Real is not an ought because the role I am to play is not expected. Instead it is a gift given by my Maker even if it was at first the markings of my parents, family, and culture.

Therefore, it is my responsibility to first own what most deeply moves me and then to live it out for the sake of others. My passion may be working on cars. It might be making delicious and nourishing meals for people who are too overwhelmed by life to cook. It is my task to know what moves me.

How, then, do I decide whether to take up playing a musical instrument or enroll in a Spanish course to prepare to go with my church to build homes in Tijuana? Or is it time to struggle with my weight by joining a health club? The church is offering training for a small-group leaders' ministry. Should I get involved or concentrate on spending more time with my kids? The rubber meets the road when a potential yes means saying a thousand noes to a legion of legitimate choices. If I learn Spanish to go on a series of short-term mission trips, I will have to say no to many other attractive opportunities that are bound to come along.

Key to making such decisions is identifying our greatest pleasure. What is our desire and passion? We find the answer as we read our tragedies and see where our character finds the greatest pleasure. We are meant to say our core yes to our most central, well-contoured passion that draws forth and reveals God's beauty. And we are meant to say no to that which has brought about the kind of harm that we can do something to stop. God has crafted our character and given us a role that will reveal something about him that no one else's story can reveal in quite the same way.

I worked with a woman in her sixties who grew up in a back-hills area of the Deep South. She was born into an illiterate Pentecostal pastor's family. This family suffered sexual abuse, alcoholism, and violence for more than one generation. This woman's abuse was so deep she seemed destined to be swallowed in the mayhem. Her story involved so much loss and shame that it brought deep pain just to hear her tell it, let alone imagine what it must have been like for her to live it. My work with her was brief, but I am privileged to see her periodically at conferences.

Today this woman is a brilliant and gifted therapist. She has battled to rescue hundreds of other delicate souls that were poisoned by the bite of abuse. She is a warrior, a saint, and a wild, hysterically funny, shrewd, kind-hearted woman. And I was privileged to be a small part of her walk toward embracing beauty. All I need to do is close my eyes to see her face. I can hear her laugh, and I know what I am meant to say yes to in my life.

I don't recall ever asking God for the privilege of working with traumatically abused men and women, yet that is what I do. I don't believe God hands out our callings like an army quartermaster dispenses a uniform, rations, and a gun to a soldier. God invites us to follow our passions even when we are unaware that they exist.

My character was formed in the midst of family violence, tension, and heartache. I came early to the calling of translation and intervention. God called me unto a family and a story of heartache, violence, and oddity. I am called to care for the angry, abused, broken people. And I know joy, the divine yes of God, in the rise of redemption from the hidden, dark, shame-filled waters of abuse.

What would I rather do: amble about life with little purpose other than seeking comfort or engage in my divine yes and no, even if doing so brings heartache? It's a choice, just as in *The Matrix,* between the red pill and the blue pill. One will quiet you and let you sleep through the terror of this world, while the other will awaken you to be a warrior fueled by the passions of redemption. You and I are meant to know the rush and the arousal of redemption.

It matters little what problem, population, or place you tackle. It only matters that something in your soul pulses with eternity to join the cast of characters that ventures to create glory and beauty out of the ashes of the Fall. It is redemption that lures you to say yes. Redemption is not narrow or limited to what some call full-time Christian service. Redemption— freeing of the soul and the body from death to life, loosening of injustice, assaulting disease, growing of crops for the hungry, comforting the dying, teaching a child to read, delivering a warm greeting to a neighbor, helping a child tie her shoe—is all about saying a divine yes to glory. And for each of us there is a script written that is contoured to our deepest passions, that reflects our core character and our truest calling. We are written to be *real,* and there is something in every heart that knows when we are and when we are not.

If we are willing to study our life, God will give us signs and clues as to our calling. If we will read our story, especially our tragedies, then we will better understand what forms our passion. And we'll be better prepared to be real as we say yes and no.

What is your passion?

Telling Your Story

Consider this idea as you think about your life: "We will not know our true self unless we can name the passions that are tied to our ideal self." Describe your ideal self in the areas of worker, friend, spouse, parent, child, citizen, and believer.

chapter five

facing the tragedy
that shapes you

The Illuminating Plot Twists of Shame and Betrayal

Why must holy places be dark places?
C. S. Lewis

Heartache awakens us to the whisper of a rumor, to a hint of the truth that we're not at home. We spend most of our life pursuing both necessity and luxury, guided by the presumption that life can be orderly and predictable if we just try hard enough. And then tragedy in some form breaks through and awakens us.

Tragedy awakens passion in a way that times of calm and blessing, pleasure and joy, cannot. The word *passion* comes from a Latin root that means "suffering." It implies intense emotion that energizes a person to move. We are moved to act when we are in pain. When we know joy, we may dance and sing, but over time joy brings the heart to rest. Tragedy, on the other hand, moves the heart to act. All passion is founded on pain, grown through risk, and marked by the decisions we make in the face of tragedy.

Tragedy introduces us to ourselves, to our deepest passions, to what it is that receives either our yes or our no. We move on an invisible track that is grooved more by passion and desire than by any other source of motivation. We do what we want even when we don't know what we want. When we opt not to do the thing we think we want, it's because a greater desire or want is at play. When we fail to act, we of course act. And the same is true of choice. Our failure to intentionally choose a course of action is no less a decision. And everything that we do is fueled by passion and moved forward by an inescapable and pulsing desire that can't be satisfied on this earth.

If I study your patterns of saying yes to this and no to the other thing, I will see the contours of your deepest passions. And if I follow the passions of your life, I will not only gain a greater sense of your past and your future, but I might hear the name that God will one day call you.

Our lives are filled with tragedy. But far more amazing, we live out our stories surrounded by an angelic host and a multitude of stories that serve to put our lives in context and give meaning to our heartaches. We must learn to read our passions in order to know the heart of God. And it is in the midst of our tragedies, both past and present, that we will see how the waters of suffering have cut our terrain and formed the contours of our character. More than anything else, tragedies shape our identity and our character.

Reading Tragedy

We begin reading the tragedy of our story when we recognize it as the rule rather than the exception. There is not a person on earth who has escaped life's pivotal, inciting incidents—incidents that are full of sadness, injustice, failure, and cruelty; incidents that require action to change or redeem them. If we are listening to another person's story, we must presume that shalom has been shattered and that s/he is on a journey to restore balance. But most of the time as we look at other lives or even our own, we fail to see the pivotal tragedies that have set into motion the plot of a person's life.

There are two primary reasons for this absence of perspective. On the one hand, some people have so many shattering moments that hearing their story is like walking through a military cemetery with tens of thousands of white crosses and Stars of David. The cemetery is so vast that it's impossible to grasp the single most important event that exposes the person's incalculable loss. On the other hand, some people have coasted through life with very little hardship. Where are the inciting incidents that define their lives? Most people have some sad and difficult moments, but often those moments occurred long ago and don't seem connected to the life the person is living today. And when we look back, many of those moments don't seem that dramatic or pivotal, so they are easily cast aside.

A woman told me with embarrassment about her longstanding discomfort with her teeth. She seldom smiled, but she was kind, and I had not noticed the absence of a wide-mouthed smile. Her elementary-school years were full of teasing and cruel remarks about her buckteeth. She is now in her sixties, still single, and she has lived a good life. But she had not taken stock of the harm done or of what she really wanted to become in the face of such long-ago hurt.

She began to take stock of her life when a friend asked her, "Why did you make every man who pursued you pay?" It was the first question about her singleness that ever pierced this woman's heart. She was kind to everyone—except a man who wanted to date her. Then she would become critical and distant, withdrawing any affection she might have shown to that point.

Not only are we apt to deny the tragedies of our past, but we also are willing to make others pay because of past hurt. We are combative toward the tragedies that shattered our shalom, or else we're blind to them or merely dismissive of them. In order to understand our passion, though, we must have access to the moment of shattering that set into motion both our core paradigm for how we see life and our core determination of how we will live it.

Tragedy shapes our deepest passions, and our passions shape who we are and what we will become. Each person living in a fallen world will encounter abandonment, betrayal, and shame. You can't avoid it, and neither can I. It's the necessary context in which we come to grips with how we will live. It is in the midst of affliction that we become our truest or most false self.

As we do battle against the tragedy of our story, we determine whom we will fight for and how we will wage the war of life. It is when we are unnamed through tragedy that we are given the ground to search and dig until we find the jewel of our identity. Betrayal can name you Worthless rather than Trusting. It can brand you Friendless when your true name is much closer to Faithful.

We lose ourselves and our identity in moments of unnaming, but we must return to those places to find ourselves and, even more so, to find God. This concept is hard to grasp because it's the opposite of what we assume to be true. We think we'll be happy if we can escape the past, but it is truer that without our past we are vacant beings with bland names and cookie-cutter stories. As we enter the places where we lost our name, we are most likely to hear the whisper of our new name—the name God will give us.

Each human story involves moments of being unnamed through abandonment, betrayal, and shame. The Bible talks about those experiences as being an orphan (a person abandoned), a stranger (a person betrayed), and a widow (a person shamed). And God reveals himself to be the Person who perfectly meets the needs of each one.

ORPHAN LONELINESS

Our heavenly Father is the only One who can rightly name us. Interestingly, in the ancient Near East, a father gave his sons and daughters their names. He created meaning in his children by the name he gave each one. The mother nurtured and grew the fruit of that meaning.

This custom did not give the father inordinate power; neither did it diminish the role of the mother. However, a father stood first in the circle of meaning. He might not complete the process, because it required the fecundity of his wife to bring a child to maturity. But the father began the process. And when he was absent, the momentum of meaning in the child's life was at best slowed or at worst accelerated off course at tragic speeds. In fact, in the ancient Near East, if a boy's father died, he lost his place, his name, and his inheritance. He became an orphan—a boy without protection, without provision, and without an identity.

An orphan in the time of the Old and New Testaments lived a dangerous and lonely existence. In a culture based on patrimony, to no longer have a name was tantamount to being a foreigner who had no rights or privileges. Orphans had to scratch out a living in a hard, unsympathetic world.

It is not that different today. A child who has lost his or her father due to death or divorce lives in the tension, if not the torture, between being named and being unnamed. *There was once a father, and he loved me. He tossed me in the air. I could feel the stubble on his chin and smell the Old Spice as I sat on his lap. I could feel the beat of his heart as I leaned against his chest. I once felt safe. But now I don't.*

A father can be lost through means other than divorce or death. Some fathers fall into their comfortable chairs, and their flickering televisions blind them to life and to their children. Others are snatched away by the allure of the road and the effort to pad their wallets. Others never speak— or never listen. Others have shamed us through neglect or abuse.

Sometimes the abuse comes in the form of being the favorite child. Jacob led a hard life as he fled from one betrayal to the other. He eventually met God, and then he walked with a limp for the remainder of his life. It's not hard to see why a beautiful and precocious son born late in life would seem like a treasure to this man. And Joseph was indeed a blessing from God in Jacob's later years. But this son also was a nuisance who disrupted the family order with his fantastical stories and dreams.

For Joseph, his father's favoritism carried the curse of death, as it does in any family where one child is esteemed more than his or her siblings. So even love—that is, a possessive and competitive counterfeit of love—can make a person an orphan. Favoritism in a family is always the basis for one child's being hated by those who did not receive the same rewards.

Granted, few people have glorious fathers. But even a child raised by a good father will likely be harmed by someone else—a pastor, a teacher, a coach, a mentor. Those "authority figures" are to mold their protégés' hearts and bodies for glory. But instead they often orphan us by their abuse, arrogance, or dismissal. It only takes one moment of abandonment to stain the cloth of glory. And we all know some form of abandonment.

There are many ways of becoming an orphan, but they all lead to the same end: a swirl of desire to touch our absent father's face and hear him speak our name. The desire is more than most of us can bear, and we turn against that ache by killing all our desire to feel safe in our father's presence.

I say this from personal experience. I was caught in a moment of emptiness several years after my stepfather died. I was watching a documentary on the fiftieth anniversary of D-day. It was overwhelming to hear veterans of World War II describe the terror and horror of landing on the Normandy beaches. My stepfather had made two landings, one at Iwo Jima and the other at Pelielu in the Pacific campaign. He was a nineteen-year-old staff sergeant. As I watched the documentary, I saw raw footage of the Normandy landing and heard the commentary of men now in their eighties, and I began to weep. The tears increased as if someone turned the faucet full blast, and finally words came out: "Thank you. Thank you." I wanted to thank my father for his courage and let him know in a way that I had never expressed to his face how much I respected and admired him.

I could easily justify why I didn't speak these words when my father was alive. He would have been silent and awkward. If tears had come to my eyes, he would have turned away and changed the subject. He was a man of his generation, and there was no room for such "sentimentality." But during the documentary, the justification melted away, and the pure desire to touch my father's face, to speak his name, seemed stronger than the fear of his defensiveness and surer than the reality of his death.

After my tears dried, I wondered out loud if I had really experienced such anguish. The pain was so real I could only handle it by questioning whether it had really happened. The tears are long gone, but the memory of that moment and my desire to speak to my father remain. I want to thank him, and his absence both in life and in death creates an ache that I want to turn off, but I can't. The desire to connect with my father increases the pain of both what I didn't have when he was living and the loss I suffered at his death. But my pain at his absence is as much about God as it is about my father. Let me explain.

God wants us to start asking important questions, and he uses our fleeting and unquenchable desire to connect with our earthly father to raise the questions we all need to face. God wants us to ask the questions of meaning: "Who am I? What am I made to be and to do? What is worth dying for?" As we ask, we begin a new journey, because we give up the superficial answers that seemed to have worked for decades.

Asking about meaning shakes the false foundation of how we get by from one day to the next. The culture that surrounds us offers answers that are meant to satisfy: You are a consumer who desperately needs a new PDA. You are a Christian father who needs to have a date night with your daughter once a week. You are a conservative or liberal who votes certain platform issues no matter who the candidate might be. You faithfully attend church and work in committees and give your time and money to good causes.

Those answers move you from today to tomorrow. But how do they accomplish that? And why do you accept the answers? Who knows? You do so because you do so. And, as the old beer commercial perceptively mocked, "Why ask why?" What did Hamlet gain by asking his simple question about being, other than getting stabbed with a poisoned dagger so he could die after a stirring soliloquy?

We flinch at the idea of asking those tough questions because we know that if we ask, the answers will change us. We will be exposed as orphans.

We will be set adrift from the authoritarian culture that serves as a surrogate father. We will never again be able to rest in the culture's arms, satisfied that it can serve as the father we never had but always desired. And being adrift, we are unnamed. *I thought I knew who I was, but now I have no idea.* Like Abraham, we leave our comfortable Ur—but only if we are willing to follow the madness of faith. As we are unnamed by the absence of our father, we find faith demanding us to begin our journey to touch the face of God.

And it is on that journey that we begin to see that we have turned to others for self-definition, safety, and companionship in order to banish the loneliness of life.

STRANGER ENVY

Many of our wounds have to do with our friends and our siblings. Friendships bring a harvest of conviviality and joy; they also can send us into exile. The psalmist laments the agony of a lost friendship.

> It is not an enemy who taunts me—
> > I could bear that.
> It is not my foes who so arrogantly insult me—
> > I could have hidden from them.
> Instead, it is you—my equal,
> > my companion and close friend.
> What good fellowship we enjoyed
> > as we walked together to the house of God.[1]

Friendships that go bad sicken the heart. The psalmist can't walk to the temple without being reminded of the conversations and joy he once knew with his friend. Worship will never be the same again. The path they shared is now stained with the blood of betrayal. His friend now wants him destroyed, if not dead. His heart feels the tremors of terror, and he wants to fly away with the wings of a dove.[2]

The loss of a friendship sends the heart into exile. It makes us aliens and strangers, wandering in a foreign land. The restaurants where we used to meet for coffee, the books we used to read and discuss, are now part of a country that will never be home again. The history of associations and connections is severed, and the stories we shared will now be told to no one. Instead they'll die the slow death of inattention and starvation.

And the death we experience in the loss of a friendship doesn't always stop with the first friend; it rampages down the slope like an avalanche. After one of my long-term friendships disintegrated, a mutual friend told me: "I can't be your friend and still be in his inner circle. Whether the gossip about you is true or false or a bit of both really doesn't matter. I don't want to know because as long as I am in his camp, it's best only to know his side." Thus, I lost *two* friends.

I was stunned by this man's honesty and also by the crude politicizing of friendship. I was dumped because my former friend was more powerful than I. My former compatriot had more to offer, so I lost a second friend. Relationships seem permanent, but they are no more solid than the ground that can be shaken by an earthquake.

Joseph was also an outcast. He was not sensitive to the hatred his brothers felt toward him, and he used his position of power and honor in a way that further alienated them. So the first chance they had, they made him pay. And Joseph became an alien and a stranger. Being cast out like that is bitter brew. The result for many is a tremor that forbids making new friends and a hardness that refuses to go to the temple again, where the former friend might be encountered. It is easier to cut the loss and sever both the memories of the past and any dreams of reconciliation.

Betrayal opens our eyes to our core loneliness. We are alone, and no matter how well we may be known by others, there is no certainty that those we sacrifice for today will love us tomorrow. Friendships are fraught with pain and the potential for betrayal.

When we feel alone, we begin to ask if there is any relationship that can survive sin. *Am I a true friend? Do I know what it is to care and abide? How am I to live with my relational failures and regrets, the current ache, the fear of what will come tomorrow?* Asking such questions opens the door for us to seek answers. At some point our asking sends us out of our comfortable conventions and compels us to look for what we are missing. Seeking is wandering with a mission but without knowing where the path leads. Hope demands that I look outside my bitterness for the sweetness I once knew in the laughter of my friend.

Our story is a face-to-face encounter with *all* of life's betrayals—not just the loss of relationship with close friends or siblings. Such losses set us on a journey, and as we wander, we awaken to being unnamed most profoundly when we suffer the loss of our lover.

WIDOW SHAME

The drama of our life begins with our father and mother: they give us our name and set the parameters of our life's meaning. The drama is furthered through relationships with friends: they bring us care, conviviality, and protection. But the most intimate and powerful drama has to do with our lover, our spouse. (And if we have never been married, a great portion of our drama relates to the issues of why we have not been pursued and chosen.)

We struggle with the heartache and desire related to being a man with a woman or a woman with a man.

One can be widowed in two different ways: death or distance. Death takes our lover to a separate realm and leaves us bereft. We cannot follow, contact, or enjoy even a moment of pleasure again with the person we love most. We are trapped in our memories of joy and our dreams of a return. A widow is caught between two worlds, past and future, which do not give up their pleasures until the day we return to the beloved.

Another form of widowhood is being married to a distant, untrustworthy spouse. There are many who sleep each night with a living corpse who will rise the next morning, brush his or her teeth, expect breakfast, and complain about the day ahead. It is onerous to imagine waking up next to a person whom you don't love and whom you know doesn't love you. This is living-death widowhood. Sadly, many marriages die while both spouses are still breathing. In most cases, in order to survive such emptiness, many give up their own drama, turn themselves over to watching other people's lives (television, sports, church, romance novels), and slip away into a vicarious fantasy life.

Also, there are single men and women who exist in perpetual widowhood. They grieve what has never been and often surrender their present to dread of the future. The (erratically or serially) promiscuous single gives his or her body to temporary partners who are committed only to their own pleasure. The result is that the most intimate gift one can offer is given to someone who is guaranteed to rip off the paper and plunder the gift with no commitment to the present or future. Sex without the prior expression of loyalty and commitment loses all meaning because it lacks memory of the past or promise of a future. It is nothing more than a random, chaotic act. In that sense, all promiscuity is a form of violence. It may well be mutually agreed upon and highly pleasurable for both participants, but it lacks trust. Therefore it is torn from commitment and promise.

And there are many singles who live with not only the loss or absence of a partner but also the memory of past violence and the anticipation of once again being misused. It is widowhood, but without the benefit of a shared past or the anticipated reunion following death.

Even the nonpromiscuous single experiences widowhood. She is single to some degree because she has not been chosen. In our couple-based world, it is agonizing to attend parties, sit at church, or go shopping and know that no one is committed to you. You realize as you climb the stairs to your apartment that no one will turn the light on for you or make sure the house is clear of intruders. When taking the car to the garage, you know that no one will help hold the mechanic accountable to not rip you off. And who will take you to work while your car is being repaired? Beyond these practical challenges, a bed has two sides, but there is only one person to take a favored spot. On countless matters, the single woman bears the same pain as a widow, but with the additional heartache of not having been chosen.

All widowhood steals the pleasure of intimacy in the present. It robs us of the connectedness to another soul whose naming of us gives us the most intimate sense of being we can find on earth. There are names my wife calls me in the course of a day that no one else on earth calls me. And there is a name—one single, hidden name—that my wife uses and that no one else will ever hear. She uses that name when there are long miles between us, and she wants me to know the depth and playfulness of her care. When she sings those syllables, I know to listen more deeply and intently because what follows will be a word from the one who has most called me to my name and who has the sweetest hints as to what my name will one day be. My wife names me more than any other person on the earth.

When I consider the prospect of her future death, I can't imagine my life afterward. I can't fathom being alive a single day in her absence. Her absence would make me suddenly deaf and blind, cut off from the truest pleasure my body and soul have known. It would take away my ability to speak. In Hebrew, the word *widow* means "to be tongue-tied." It is to lose the ability to speak, for in that loss what else would one ever say but "take me away from this loss"?

The shame of widowhood is that when we are alone, we can't cover the nakedness of desire. As a widow we pulse with memory of what we once enjoyed but will never again give or receive. I spoke to a widow in her seventies who told me that she still puts two cups out in the morning before the coffee is brewed because that is what she did for more than fifty years with her husband. Tears began to roll down her etched face, and she said, "I know he is gone, but my hands so often forget." I told her I hoped her hands never stopped remembering his presence. And then she turned away, blushing. She was flush with a desire undiminished by years of loss. Such is the risk and the weight of love. It calls us to live naked and alone but awash with desire for the return of the beloved.

In the presence of love, we are rightly named. In the presence of love, we find our truest story. But it is only when we are unnamed by absence, betrayal, and ambivalence—as we engage our father, friends, and lover—that we are laid bare, made naked and open to the call of a new name and a new story. We must be unnamed before we can be renamed to know our true name and story. When we are named Orphan, Stranger, or Widow, we begin the journey of finding our true name. Will we defy the tragedy of becoming an orphan, a stranger, and a widow by saying yes to the passions that God has put in us? To turn away from, rather than embrace and learn from, tragedy is a double loss. We lose not only in the original harm, but we add to that harm by closing our heart.

Whatever has broken our heart is meant to arouse our anger. It is from anger that we gain the ability to shout, "No!" We are to say no to the harm that befell us so that it does not add to the cycle of violence that harms others. If we face our tragedies with an open heart, we will become more tender toward ourselves and others. Tenderness gives us the freedom to speak yes to those who ache and who need the kind touch of our care. Tragedy prepares us to become who we are meant to be.

I find my name and story when I struggle with tragedy. I was unnamed by tragedy, and either I will lose my name completely because of it or I will find my truest name as I meet it face to face. The tragedies of life, small and large, carve contours in our character that draw us to a different way of living, one that God intends to both use and transform.

Tragedy asks: "Are you willing to do battle with what has broken your heart?" And it calls out: "Will you let God transform you in the midst of your struggle?" Both questions set the course for the kind of character and calling God has written for our life.

Telling Your Story

At what points in your life has God remained silent? Make a list of instances when you have been
- an orphan, fatherless and unprotected;
- a stranger, alone and without a friend;
- a widow, rejected or not chosen.

chapter six

getting caught by your calling

Revealing God Through the Themes of Your Life

God acts in history and in your and my brief
histories not as a puppeteer who sets the scene and
works the strings but rather as the great director
who no matter what role fate casts us in conveys to
us somehow from the wings, if we have our eyes,
ears, hearts open and sometimes even if we don't,
how we can play those roles in a way to enrich and
ennoble and hallow the whole vast drama of things
including our own small but crucial parts in it.

FREDERICK BUECHNER

The day had arrived and a decision had to be made: would I accept a job offer to teach at a respected seminary, or would I become part of the team that was starting a new graduate school in Seattle? My wife and I had spent weeks tossing around various options, and it boiled down to a choice between safety and madness. The established seminary offered security, a good salary, and the opportunity to teach the courses that I wanted. The chance to start a new school was ridiculous. We needed to raise three hundred thousand dollars just to find out if we would fail.

I had reached the moment where a commitment needed to be finalized. Becky brought the discussion to a close when she said, "You've never had a normal life. Why start now?" In a matter of seconds, my mind flitted from how we met, to how I was seduced to go to seminary, to how I met Larry Crabb and went into counseling, to how Larry and I began a counseling program, to the events that had drawn Becky and me to this decision point. For whatever reason, my mind landed on the first sermon I heard after becoming a Christian.

I was a troubled twenty-year-old who had been involved in illicit pharmaceutical sales for a number of years. The small cartel with whom I worked had arranged to sell drugs from a new supplier. I learned after the fact that the drugs would be coming from sources connected with organized crime. All of a sudden I had gone from the status of middle-class, mom-and-pop drug czar to the "big time." And the big time involved carrying guns, buying judges and police, and threatening undisciplined dealers. I wanted out, and I knew that could mean forfeiting my life. I can't explain why I had the strength to slip the bonds of that world, but I did. I knew that if I died I would go to hell. More precisely, I knew that *if* there was a hell, I was certainly going there.

Somewhere in the recesses of my soul I believed in God, but the other

98 percent of my being thought the whole business of God was absurd. Death lay ahead eventually, no matter what I decided to do, so I said, "Fine," to God. That was the entirety of my prayer: "Fine." If it's true, then fine; if not, I didn't have much to lose.

I knew the gospel well because my best friend, Tremper, had discussed it with me many times. I had watched people come to know Jesus and had gone to a few Bible conferences and even to the campus of the seminary I eventually attended. I knew the basic beliefs of Christianity well, but it was not for me. Yet I was glad it was true for my best friend.

The night I came to faith I had ingested a sizable dose of hallucinogens earlier in the day, so I was fairly fried. I felt profoundly uncomfortable walking into that small Presbyterian church in the country. People were friendly and warm. Tremper and I sat off to one side about midway between coming and going. I felt relieved I was on the end of the row so that if I needed to run, I'd have full access to an escape route.

The service began. At certain times people would stand, and I couldn't figure out what prompted the shift from sitting to standing. They read and spoke back to the dude up front. They sang, and then they would bow their heads and close their eyes as if the whole thing had been choreographed. Was I missing some hand signals or a secret command from the front? Clearly some time would be required for me to figure out this scene.

Then the guy in the robe began to talk. We opened the black books in front of us, and he read and then talked about what he had read. I didn't bother to read, nor did I listen. But somehow I heard him mention Balaam's ass. My ears came alive with curiosity.

He talked about how Balaam's ass had spoken to Balaam. I was freaked out. I glanced around and noticed that no one seemed at all concerned about this bizarre revelation. Halfway through the sermon the preacher switched and started saying, "Balaam's donkey." I was so relieved I nearly fell out of my seat.

In fact, I was so relieved I thought I would cry. A talking animal was just fine. Under the influence of LSD, I had often heard animals talk, but the thought of going through my religious life with talking body parts seemed more than any human ought to bear. Somehow, as unlikely as it might sound, I came to faith that night.

Faith gradually became central to my life, and years later my wife and I were faced with the decision to make a career move. Why would the scene in that rural Presbyterian church come to mind as Becky commented, "You've never had a normal life. Why start now?" Stories inform story. Becky and I were in the middle of a new, developing story. And old stories returned to help us make the decision that would be at the core of our new story. The decision was made. The hard work of weighing options, praying, and seeking counsel was crucial in sorting out the issues that mattered to us most, but the decision crystallized when Becky read my life, then identified and embraced the other-than-normal path we have been called to walk.

The future is meant to be written in light of the patterns of the past. We can't predict the future, but we can read the patterns of the past to see how God has marked us for his purposes. He uses the past to open our future. As we learn to read patterns, we gain an understanding of our calling.

Reading Patterns

Becky and I and our friend Christie were traveling together on a half-day road trip. Our conversation was pleasant and free. After talking about various matters, my wife asked us both: "If you were a letter of the alphabet, what would it be?" Her question struck me as a monumental waste of time, a silly icebreaker for a threesome who had been through fire, storm, and calamity together. We didn't need to break any ice; we had been broken by more ice moments than an Antarctic explorer. But Christie, to my chagrin, jumped in with both feet. She added, "Before we answer for ourselves, why don't we say what letter we consider each other to be?" I was irked but outnumbered, so I played along.

We made guesses about one another and then explained why we had made our choice. It turned out to be a fascinating conversation, but then it was my turn to be associated with a letter of the alphabet. When my wife said, "X," Christie began to laugh because she had chosen the same letter. My wife chose it because of the word *X-treme*. Christie chose it because she sees me as a person who lives on the border, at the crossroads, always pressing limits and calling others to cross to another side.

I laughed, but I felt caught and exposed. I am often more extreme than others. I live more in the drama of intensity and the crisis of decision than in reflective meditation. I felt the blush of being known and honored, albeit with the sense that both women were saying I am enjoyed yet it is best to take me in small doses. We will not read the patterns of our past unless we have data from the present. And the data can't come with fullness and accuracy until they come from others. We simply can't see our own face.

If we want to know the truth about ourselves, we must be in a relational dialogue. That's how God has made us. We must be avid, curious, and open if we are to learn who we are. We must listen to the wind that wafts through a conversation when someone asks, "Have you always been so intense?" or "You seem so sure of yourself—don't you ever doubt?" or "How come you seem to always hang back and let others speak before offering your opinion?"

Throughout our lifetime, all sorts of people have named us. Some of the naming has been cruel, designed to imprison us in shame. Others have spoken to us with the hope that their kiss and compliment would win them access to something they want from us. Still others, innocently or inadvertently, have named us, and those data are best given sober consideration. Stop now and think for a moment about the observations others have made about you. What are they? How do you react to these observations? Do you find truth there?

Add to that data more intentional feedback—input that you seek out. It is imperative to hear from those who know, love, and respect you. How do they see you, both at your best and at your worst? How do they experience you when you are hurt, angry, afraid, lonely, confident, jubilant, and at rest? If you will listen to the words of others' experience of you, I guarantee you will be surprised and humbled.

CONNECTING THE DOTS

If you collect the data from a number of different observers, you will begin to notice that certain words, phrases, and concepts overlap. It is this overlap, the coincidence of common characteristics, that sketches an initial pattern. Once you own the pattern as at least somewhat true of who you are, then it's wise to look at the past and ask, "How did this pattern come to exist?"

So explore the overlap of observations. But remember that some of the words, phrases, and images used to describe you will be inconsistent. There is a simple reason for apparent or explicit contradiction: we are complex, inconsistent, and contradictory beings. We love and we hate. We sacrifice for others and we are self-absorbed. We are a mass of consistent inconsistencies. Therefore, as we turn to the process of reading our patterns, we must embrace the reality that there are as many gaps in our being as there are dots to be connected. As we read what is both consistent and inconsistent, we begin to gain the true measure of ourselves.

Dots and Gaps

Let's assume you have entered into significant conversations with a handful of friends, especially your spouse and children. You have heard, perhaps with some emotion, descriptions of what it's like to be around you at your best and at your worst. You now have a stock of data, and you've moved beyond defensiveness, doubt, and dismissal. You have collated the data and embraced much of it as likely being a true description of who you are. What do you do now?

It's time to connect the dots and plunge into the gaps. Connecting the dots means linking the words and phrases into a coherent pattern, no matter how flattering or disconcerting it might be. The gaps are the words or phrases that are anomalies, the observations that seem foreign or contradictory to the larger picture others have of you. In reading your patterns—both in terms of consistency and inconsistency—you begin to get an inkling of your life theme.

Patterns That Reveal Themes

Listen to your life. It will give you countless words that describe your way of being, relating, and engaging others. These words will help you identify your character and your role in life.

Listen to your stories. They reveal a pattern of roles that you've played throughout your life. Without question there will be discrepancies and mind-boggling contradictions. There is evolution and transformation, but the being that a person was at age three still has some overlap with the inner world of that same person at age ninety-three. A coherent sense of self lasts over a lifetime, and what is retained over a lifetime speaks to the unique role or character you are to play out on God's stage. What lasts, yet grows and matures to an even greater glory, reveals your thematic calling.

A theme is a unifying idea or motif repeated throughout a story. Begin by noticing what repeats and then note how it unifies the complexities of a story into a coherent whole. A theme is not merely the core point or moral of a story. In fact, if a story or life can be summarized as a moral, then it has lost its intrigue. In other words, a story that has a moral doesn't reflect the inverted, complex, surprising, and scandalous story of the gospel. A gospel life will be rich, complex, contradictory, and surprising until the end. That's what makes it real and true. That's what makes *you* real.

A theme is also the meaning of a life that, when put into words, always needs to be rewritten to better state what is true. A theme can be spoken, but it is presumptuous to think we can codify a story, let alone an entire life. In fact, it's almost completely the opposite. As we explore the stories of our life, we gradually sense the development of a theme, the growth of significance. We feel ourselves caught up in a vital process in which meaning emerges from experience. In the end, that sense of deepening discovery in experience makes our life interesting to us. It is this way with all real stories. Fiction is never the mere illustration of an idea. It is the created image of the very life process by which we feel ourselves moving toward meaning in our own experience.[1]

A life theme is not our mission, moral, or purpose. It is the significance of our life as seen by those who are close enough to sense how our life either reveals or fails to make known the character of God.

Rightly Reading Your Life Theme

I know a woman whose life mission is to make God known by her efforts to call people to come alongside those who have lost the safety and joy of their home as a result of domestic violence. Nancy Murphy, the director of both the Northwest Family Life Counseling Center and the Domestic Violence Advocacy program at Mars Hill Graduate School, is intimately familiar with the carnage of abuse. Her first husband began abusing her on the second day of their honeymoon. The abuse lasted for ten years.

The story Nancy tells is marked with the tragedy of silence and shame, denial and desperate hope. She remained in the marriage because of the conviction that God offered her no alternative but to remain faithful and submissive. As the violence against her children grew, she eventually fled her native Canada and began a sojourn of education and personal healing. That journey resulted in her leading one of the foremost faith-based treatment centers in the nation. Her story is more compelling than any Hollywood drama, but in stating what she does, I have not named her life theme or her calling. What we do for a living, or in a ministry, or in family life or friendship is merely the context for our calling. I don't believe anyone has the calling to be president of a corporation, founder of a ministry, or director of a counseling center. Those are fine jobs and sometimes careers, but our calling is not what we do—it's how we do it.

Nancy grew up on the west coast of Vancouver Island. It is a rugged, desolate, isolated part of the world. One of the few ways to move along the coast—one of the most inhospitable shorelines in the world—is by boat. Nancy grew up with her brothers and sisters on a fifty-foot boat with her parents who were missionaries to the native inhabitants of the island coast.

Nancy didn't realize she was Caucasian until she was nine. Her soul and worldview are Native Canadian.

Native Canadians do not set one another apart by giving awards or acknowledging outstanding achievement. To make one person greater is to make many less. Yet Nancy is a gentle, soft-spoken, down-to-earth, hilariously witty, wise, and bold woman, and for me to write those words about her nearly kills her. She allows me to say so only because it reveals something she prizes more than her privacy or comfort—the gospel.

Now, domestic violence is not a popular subject. It evokes terrifying images. It also tends to attract advocates for change who are angry and impatient to see things happen. This shameful topic is further ignited by inflammatory activists. The result is that the larger population is alienated rather than enlisted to come alongside those who are broken by domestic violence.

So, in her line of work, Nancy is a conundrum. She is gentle and passionate. She is highly professional but always a warm and approachable human being. She has spoken before the joint houses of Congress and the Helsinki Conference to address the relationship between domestic violence and sexual trafficking. Normally, those who are granted such vaunted pulpits take on an air of scientific objectivity and dispassionate distance, but Nancy addresses the issues with passion and humanity. She invites people to both suffer and hope, to dream and risk. And she does so with a genteel depth that sneaks through defenses on both sides of the debate.

I know no one else who more richly lives the Beatitudes—blessed are the broken, the weak, and the poor, for they will not only be comforted, but they will rule the earth. Nancy's life theme is this: the broken and the foolish will triumph because of the wild and unpredictable paradox of love. Nancy and her husband, Tom, are wild and dangerous people whose life theme reveals God's intention and delight to destroy violence through kindness. Is it Nancy's calling to combat domestic violence? The answer is yes. She counsels, trains, educates, directs research, and implores others to open their eyes to the horror in order to see in it—and beyond it—to the hope of the glory of God.

But is Nancy's calling really to domestic violence? I believe the full answer is complicated. Nancy's calling is to domestic violence but also to a far greater goal: to invite others into the mystery of God's kindness. If you listen to her story, you hear all that she experienced throughout the horrific ordeal of domestic abuse. Yet her life theme reveals the odd hand of God who uses the most unexpected people to bring about the most unusual transformations.

A life theme sets the trajectory of our life, and that trajectory is woven into the role we are to play. The specific tasks are but the open door we walk through to step onto God's stage. It is no wonder, then, that there are as many life themes as there are people. However, all the truest themes have to do with what each of us uniquely reveals about God's character. Our calling is to reveal God through the themes he has woven into our character. The questions that relate to where (place), what brokenness to confront (problem), with whom (population), and how (process) are largely left to our own choice and talents. The fact that a person is born a Caucasian Native Canadian on the west coast of Vancouver Island doesn't mean that person won't someday be testifying before both houses of Congress. Location, timing, nationality, gender, and age don't limit the creativity or humor of God.

Once we begin to read our life, then we are called by God to do more: we are called to mess with our story. We are called to write our destiny and edit our writing in community with others for the sake of an even better and truer story. But first we must have some sense of the direction our story is meant to move. We must at least catch a whisper of our calling.

GOD'S CALL: WHAT IT IS NOT

God calls us, which means we must listen and respond. God calls us to tasks and to service, but most important, he calls us into relationship with him. But when most people use the word *calling,* they're usually referring to a to-do list, a job offer, or a wish list. The truth about calling, however, is that it has little to do with any of these.

It's Not a To-Do List

Our calling is not a list of things God wants us to get done, yet most of us have some affinity for lists. We find it helpful to break down our complex goals into bite-size tasks that, taken together, add up to a realized objective. For example, when asked how I write a book, I say, "I have no idea. I have never done it, nor am I capable of doing it." Writing a book is an impossible task, but it is not that difficult to write twelve chapters. The person who has not learned the skill of segmenting his or her life goals and tasks is at a severe disadvantage, because everything will look too big to do.

So while creating to-do lists is a necessary skill, it is not what God calls us to do. His calling involves doing, but we are seldom called to do a single or even a central task. What he calls us to do is in accord with a larger task—that of being. We are not what we do, but we do become like whom we serve. This process may seem complex, but it's actually quite simple. An excellent pianist can play the notes of a song without playing it with passion. A superb tennis player can hit every stroke as well as a pro but never break into the top one hundred. Why? It's the issue of heart. And the issue of the heart always has to do with whom or what we worship.

Even in the animal kingdom, a story like *Seabiscuit* revolves around the intangible but observable issue of heart. A browbeaten little horse is sold for a pittance because it is deemed deficient. A wise handler slowly draws out its strengths and uses its wounds to engender a ferocity that is unbeatable when the horse is ridden with wisdom.

I don't question this story. It is the same in each person's story. God speaks with ferocity about the issues of our heart:

I am sick of your sacrifices.... Don't bring me any more burnt offerings! I don't want the fat from your rams or other animals. I don't want to see the blood from your offerings of bulls and rams and goats.... Learn to do good. Seek justice. Help the oppressed. Defend the orphan. Fight for the rights of widows.[2]

I hate all your show and pretense—the hypocrisy of your religious festivals and solemn assemblies. I will not accept your burnt offerings and grain offerings. I won't even notice all your choice peace offerings. Away with your hymns of praise! They are only noise to my ears. I will not listen to your music, no matter how lovely it is. Instead, I want to see a mighty flood of justice, a river of righteous living that will never run dry.[3]

God commanded his people to offer burnt offerings, and then he said, "They make me sick." He wants us to live with a heart of passion for justice—period. Religious deeds, be it prayer, fasting, giving, sacrifice, song, or dance, turn God's stomach when we do them without a heart for right-eousness. And living out righteousness is no less than creating a holy, beau-tiful, sacred space for glory to grow. God doesn't give us a to-do list; instead he calls our heart to holiness and justice.

It's Not a Job Offer

Most people understand calling as God's calling us to a specific job. Indeed, God called adolescent Jeremiah to preach of his coming judgment. And God called Paul (then named Saul) to serve the very people that he, blinded by zeal, had been trying to destroy. God calls us to certain tasks and jobs, but he doesn't do so because we are uniquely suited to do them. He calls us to the task or job because we are weak, broken, and ill-equipped for the task.

I don't believe anyone is called to a job or a profession. My calling in life is not to be a writer, therapist, speaker, teacher, trainer, or administra-tor. My calling is to walk through any door God gives me in order to reveal his glory. If I'm a graduate-school president, it's for a season, but my life lasts for eternity. If I am a physician or an auto mechanic, it is no different: I am called by God not for a mere season or reason but for an eternity to reveal his glory. What is my calling? It is to make known something about God that is bound to my unique face, name, and story. It is to reveal God through my character.

It's Not a Wish List

God is not in the business of satisfying our top fifty dreams. When my daughter was in her first semester of college, she was assigned the task of coming up with fifty things she wanted to do in life. I loved the list she made. I wish I had been compelled to do the same when I was that age.

Though, of course, it's never too late. The dilemma is that we find no one in Scripture who was asked to think in those terms. It's an assignment that makes sense only in a Western, capitalistic, middle- or upper-middle-class culture. Imagine the answer of an immigrant family: "We want to find a job and obtain food, clothing, shelter, and education."

My daughter's list included pleasure and sacrifice, growing and learning, building and tearing down, relationship and ideals. She did a beautiful job of identifying what she really wants to do, but I told her, "God is not in the business of helping you succeed at achieving your dreams—even ones that involve sacrifice for his purposes." In fact, I believe he is most committed to dissolving and re-creating our dreams. God births dreams in us and then allows the desire to move us; it is in the pursuit of our dreams that we encounter tragedy and meet the deeper desires that only loss and heartache can reveal.

What deepest desire of our being does God call us to discover? It is no other love and no other one but him. We are called to reveal God through the themes and dreams he has woven into our heart. Therefore, to know our calling, we must come to name the unique trajectory of our story.

Getting Caught by Your Calling

We begin with our stories, always. So read and reread your story. In due season, some of the patterns and the trajectory of your life will begin to appear through the fog. At first there will be only a shape, but with time, prayer, and reflection, you will see the contours of your path come into focus. This is not a mere intellectual exercise.

We don't find our calling; it finds us. We may catch our calling as it hurtles toward us, but mostly we are caught in its web long before we recognize its existence. We are actor-writers of our character, but most of us sense we are discovering something that has been given to us far more than it is something we are creating. It is both/and, of course. We both discover and create. It is this dual perspective that allows us to ask: "What moves me? To what and to whom am I to say yes? How will I follow the unfathomable desires of my heart?"

God gives us desire and meaning. They are inside us alongside our calling, without any effort on our part to create them. When it comes to being caught by my calling, my options are simple: Whom will I serve (the population)? In what locale will I serve that community (the place)? In that community and in that place, what portion of the Fall will I face (the problems)? And what means will I use to address those problems (the process)? Our calling in life is always tied to population, place, problems, and process.

God may have helped you gain a sense of your calling by linking you first to one of these Ps well before he began to illuminate your story, theme, and calling. For instance, he may have built into you a great passion for Hispanic people and culture. Or perhaps mountains have captured your imagination since the vacations your family took to Vail. Either way, your heart was drawn to the mystery and magic of something particular.

Ask some questions of yourself. Why does your heart ache every time you see an advertisement for the Special Olympics? There may be no one in your life who has a developmental disability, but when a ministry for children with disabilities begins in your church, you are haunted. Or perhaps you long ago discovered that you could outwork most mere mortals. You may not be a genius, but you have the gift of perseverance. You can handle details and create order and beauty out of chaos. Your gift marks you as a life-giving presence for many who can create new ideas but couldn't administrate themselves out of paper bag.

You are gifted. You are called. You are telling a story. The clearer you can be about yourself, the further you will be on the journey of catching and being caught by your calling. And the moment you say yes to a population, a place, a problem, and a process—you have been seized by your calling.

Telling Your Story

As you listen to your life, you will hear "countless words that describe your way of being, relating, and engaging others. These words will help you identify your character and your role in life." What do the themes and patterns of your life reveal about God? What wrongs do you dream of righting? What good do you dream of growing?

writing your

writing your destiny

Take Up Pen and Paper and Follow God

If we could see. If we could read the Letter. If,
seated on high, amidst the authors of our destinies,
we could read the book of our life. Which is
written. Already written, finished. But we shall
never know our story. We are only characters in it.
And to think that there will be readers of our book.

HÉLÈNE CIXOUS

Most Americans were riveted to the television after the terrorist attacks of
September 11, 2001. Within a day the news media started following the
stories of relatives who posted pictures of missing loved ones on walls near

the collapsed World Trade Center. For a brief period, we became a nation of stories. As tragic and heart-wrenching as this event was, it became more real and personal when we saw the faces and heard the stories of those who had perished and those who were left bereft.

As horrific as news reports are when accidents or deliberate acts of violence kill and maim scores of people, the stories seldom move us unless we are given access to at least one individual's story. It is nearly impossible to feel someone's pain if we don't know that person's story.

Similarly, it is impossible to enter the pain of our own life unless we know our story. The preceding section of this book invited you to plunge into your story and become acquainted with how you've been written by your tragedies and your family roles. When reading your story, you should have recognized certain patterns and themes that compel you to say yes and no to various options in life. I pray that you have begun to feel more intrigue and sorrow for yourself and your story as you see the dimensions of how God has shaped you.

At this point it's appropriate to ask: "What do I do with chapters that I feel are too painful, the chapters I hate?" We all have chapters that make little sense and have not yet been seen in the soft light of redemption. Coming to love your own life requires you to believe that the past was God's will, that the already completed chapters were ultimately written for both his glory and your participation in his redemption. Though we can never comprehend his will regarding atrocities and evil, we simply know he is neither the author of sin, nor does anything happen that thwarts his ultimate purposes. He uses pain and brokenness, just as he uses shalom.

God writes our life from the foundation of the earth. But he doesn't let us glimpse the outcome of the story until long after we have joined him in coauthoring our life and then, ultimately, have met him face to face. In this life, we can know God's will primarily by looking back at what has already happened. We know that God is sovereign and nothing is beyond his sight, but does that truth really equip us to love *everything* that is written in our life?

We can love our past—even the parts we avoid and regret—only if we understand that our story is written for the benefit of others' stories in the future. We can truly love our life only when we see our story birth new and more glorious stories.

Interpreting your life—seeing the contours of meaning formed by what already has happened—is the first step in learning to love your life. A second step is necessary: you must now begin writing your life, since doing so brings a greater sensitivity as you face your heartache. Writing your life also brings deeper awe as you see what God has done to redeem you and how he uses your story in the lives of other people. This is why God invites you to take up your pen and follow him.

Taking Up Your Pen

We are called to hold our past together with our future; the enormity of this task is weighty. We are to take up our pen and follow the story that has already been told in order to write the story that is yet to be revealed. The implications for writing our life are enormous. Putting words on a piece of paper helps us to see with greater force the reality of our story. God has already revealed himself in and through our story. So we must write in light of what has been revealed regarding our theme and calling. Yet we can't look just to the past; we must also face the unrevealed future. We are called to see the past as given and the future as unmade and aching to be written.

If I am to write my destiny, then I must acknowledge that much was written before I arrived on this earth and that a whole lot was composed after my birth that I didn't write but instead was written for me. Yet I am frighteningly free to write as I desire, because God has written me to be fully responsible for my story.

God doesn't treat us like marionettes, pulling our strings so that we amble to a podium with glasses pushed up on our head and one pant leg tucked into the top of a boot. He doesn't treat us like plastic toys that are shuffled onto the stage and then thrown back into the toy box when he finishes his game.

We are wondrously interdependent beings who are called to write our one and only life in the light of God's glory. Does he tell us how we are to write our story? No. Does he speak? Yes. Does he speak often enough and clearly enough that we can ask him in each moment to tell us what to write? No. He speaks enough to remind us that he exists, but ambiguously enough to put us in the position of operating with faith and not sight. The process of writing our story will be filled with uncertainty, risk, and the tension of a story not yet explained.

As we write our story, however, there are signs that give us direction— starting with the dreams God has planted in our heart. God calls us to dream, plan, and write. We need not fear that we will get ahead or behind or sideways of his authoring of our life. He tells us:

> We can gather our thoughts, but the LORD gives the right answer. People may be pure in their own eyes, but the LORD examines their motives. Commit your work to the LORD, and then your plans will succeed. The LORD has made everything for his own purposes, even the wicked for punishment.... We can make our plans, but the

LORD determines our steps.... We may throw the dice, but the
LORD determines how they fall.[1]

The sovereign Lord will not be thwarted by ill motives, wayward plans, or the scheming of the unrighteous. He rules over the universe, and he even uses evil to accomplish his plan. But God's sovereignty is not an invitation to passivity. Instead, it is a call to wise and risky creativity. We must plan, and he will direct. The call is clear: we are to dream, plan, and write in accord with the prompting and urging of his Spirit. This means that we are to write in accord with the passions and themes God has written into our story.

FOLLOWING YOUR DREAMS

Your dreams are either an escape or an entry; there is no middle ground. Either you dream to get away from the day-to-day grind, the unresolved past, or the uncertain future, or you dream of ways to enter the fray for a greater good than your own. Of course, it is not wrong to dream of a long-awaited trip to Europe. It is not wrong to dream and wish for a college degree or a new fly rod. But all of our dreaming, whether grand or mundane, is either a wished-for flight back into Eden or an anticipation of the coming Eden.

The dream God gives us—the dream we are to write—is the one that draws forth our most passionate yes and no. Whatever has wounded us most deeply will be a part of what causes us to shout, "No!" And whatever has brought us the deepest joy and delight will steer us toward what we are called to bless and welcome with our heartfelt, "Yes!"

Our dreams are seldom linear or unambiguous. If you were sexually abused, it may not mean that you will spend your life saying no to that harm. Instead you might direct your anger into a desire to say no to bullies and to the misuse of power against the vulnerable. Your story may not cause you to say yes to counseling others who have been abused, but it will enlarge your joy in watching the underdog win and seeing those who were discounted and violated given a voice and new power.

Our deepest dreams are always about righting wrong and growing good. It's that simple. What wrong are you meant to stop? What good are you uniquely designed to grow? We are not meant to be happy when we reach a personal goal unless that dream is attached to the greater good of others.

Your dream, built on the passion of a single yes—perhaps "I love to teach the Bible"—must move you to throw the dice and let God bring up the numbers he wishes. The dream may be as simple as starting a neighborhood Bible study. Or your dream may be, "I love the grease and grime of working on cars," which leads you to take the risk of advertising that you're available to help widows, single women, and mechanically disinclined men gain a sense of mastery over their vehicles. Dreaming gets you into the steamy reality of life: naming your dream, making a plan, and then jumping into the water.

Any plans that spring forth from your dream eventually need to answer four core questions, which we will explore in the next few pages.

Who Am I to Serve?

Deep dreams are not about getting away to an isolated island in the balmy South Seas. Nor are our deepest dreams to climb Mount Everest or make a million dollars. If our deepest dreams aren't about other people, then we have settled for mere power and accomplishment—the self-absorption of narcissism. Our deepest and truest dreams must bring good to someone who is without justice, reconciliation, or hope. The population that we are written to serve may include many different kinds of people, but it is probably focused on a few. It is likely centered on a distinct group of people that may be bound by a particular race, nationality, region, or need. We must always be willing to go further than our own group and pursue the passions that take us into other groups of people—dirt-bike racers, church choirs, abused women, and so forth. We must dream dreams that are connected to a specific population.

Where Am I to Be?

This is the place aspect of a dream. We all are bound by space and time. I may be able to fly around the world, but every night I must sleep in a single place, not many. What is the primary context where I serve the people I am called to love? This place has an address or locale; therefore it is bound to the customs of a certain city or region. We all are bound up in our location.

The "place" question requires a choice that limits us. As much as we would like to keep all our options open, we can't. One choice to serve in a particular place closes down other options. Of course the one choice will open a vista of new choices, but each resulting decision again says no to more than it says yes to.

What Burden Am I to Bear?

Everyone is called to battle some unique effects of the Fall. For each of us, there is a problem in this world that is meant to first bring us to tears and intensify our anger and then bring joy to our soul when it is even temporarily subdued.

Answering the people question and the place question helps determine the problem we will address. For example, if we choose to serve those in a Baptist congregation in rural Mississippi that is populated by the wealthiest of the community, we will face different needs than if we choose to start an office-supply store in a growing suburban enclave in the Midwest. People in one place have different needs than a group in another locale, even if the two groups live only several miles apart.

The needs you are called to serve—financial, physical, psychological, legal, spiritual, relational, creative, intellectual, recreational—are bound tightly to gifts that God has enabled you to develop. Some of the skill sets you've developed may be things that bore you. You might be an administrative whiz but hate the tedium of working in an office shuffling papers. This usually is not an issue of despising your skills or gifts but rather a failure to use them well in a world that deeply matters to you.

Also, your gifts change, and God might prompt you to try out new areas of your giftedness in different seasons of your life. An excellent salesman, for instance, may find after many years that his talent to persuade and inform leads him to work as an educator or to start his own business instead of working for a company. All of these considerations influence us as we choose the problem we will address.

How Am I to Engage?

Answering the process question means defining how you will engage your dream. As you pursue your dream in a particular place with a defined population, addressing a problem resulting from the Fall, you bring something unique to the circumstances at hand. How you engage a person, situation, or problem is distinct. You bring your own way of being to bear on all that you do.

God wants us to relieve suffering, pursue justice, facilitate reconciliation, and free the heart to love, but he desires for us to do so in a way that reveals his character. It is not enough just to do well for others or to do things well.

We must do well in our unique way in order to reveal the vast creativity of a God who loves to bring change through the most unlikely channels.

Therefore our way of engagement may be to pray, administrate, teach, or serve. Or it could be to juggle, sing, mime, or paint. Or lead, confront, repair, or nurture. Each of us will do what we do with a style that reveals something about God in a way that no one else can.

Case in point. My daughter Amanda is tender, artful, and quirky. She tends to be relatively scattered and disconnected from a great many details of life. But she is widely read, philosophically bent, and more knowledgeable about the issues of the global sex trade than most adults. She is a formidable force with a vivacious presence. I recall once watching her point her finger at the chest of a quaking date, excoriating his weak arguments against theism, only to then see her laugh, pat him on the shoulder, and let him open the door so they could go on their date. I thought to myself, *He is going to be taken on quite an adventure tonight.*

●

The four questions we've looked at address the issues of population, place, problem, and process. We must answer these questions, but we can't expect the answers to be clear and straightforward. We may know that the population we are to serve is orphaned children. But where are they? And what dimension of their struggles are we uniquely written to address? By what means are we to enter the fray? Clarity in one area may be accompanied by ambiguity in the other three areas. But the guarantee with regard to all four questions is that an answer in just one will get us more engaged with God. And that's how we find our future—by reading and loving and writing our story for the sake of others.

YOUR TWO-EYED FUTURE

We write our future with one eye on the horizon and the other eye on the particulars that are closest to us. We see close up and far away, but we can't see both simultaneously or with equal clarity. Why? Because we're limited by our focus. But if we are to survive even a short trip to the grocery store, we must alternate often between a focus on the close up and the distant.

Most days our focus is primarily on what is before us, but few of our decisions are made solely on the basis of the moment. If I am crossing a street, my timing will almost always be based on what is physically present at that moment. But most other decisions throughout the day are calibrated by a longer distance. Do I respond to an e-mail invitation now or wait until this evening after I can talk it over with my wife? And when I talk to my wife about the e-mail regarding plans for the weekend, I will take into account how much work I think I can get done on this book because the due date is only four months away. So my response to today's e-mail invitation is loosely tied to a deadline that is still months away. We are often alternating between the close up and the far away.

Whether we realize it or not, our immediate decisions are tied to how we conceive the future. Do I buy a bigger home or put the money aside for retirement? Do I add to my busy life the demands of going to graduate school or remain in a job that pays the bills even though I shudder at the thought of doing this same job ten years from now? We move fluidly between the present and the future in the daily decisions of life.

Likewise, as we write our present and our future, we must alternate between the close up and the horizon. As complex as this process may sound, the big story of the future shapes how we write the present. And the present story is constantly limiting or expanding how we write the larger story of tomorrow and the day after. Our story is like a book, and the present stories are the scenes that make up a chapter. The two foci of present and future must continually be viewed in light of each other.

THE BIG STORY: THEME AND DESIRE

The big story reveals the why of your life: what is it that you reveal about God? Obviously this focus requires the eyes of hope so that you are able to see what can't be seen. You must imagine things that are beyond the scope of probability. To dream that you will achieve a few major goals is not enough. As you write your story, you must keep in mind that the glory of a single human life is meant for more than what is likely. Plans to travel and explore or to study and learn are not enough. Our dreams must reveal the unimaginable—that we will reflect the character and glory of God into the lives of other people.

It's time now to go beyond simple dreams and construct a personal mission statement. This exercise is far closer to authoring the future than merely entertaining a series of goals. A mission statement is a telescope to help you see a horizon not visible to the naked eye. A good mission statement takes years to form and can't be finalized without the hard work of reading your past and imagining your future. Developing a mission statement requires unearthing your desire, articulating your passion, and following the bent of your life story as God has written it. Authoring the story of the rest of your life requires that you form a personal mission statement.

Mission statements must be approached carefully. They can too easily miss the mark by sounding like grand visions and being so abstract they fail to give shape to the future. Worse, they can name a generic future that has no guts or glory. Check the Web sites of a few organizations that you respect and read their mission statements. Does the mission statement move you? Does it tell you on what the organization is willing to stake its existence, pin its hopes, and focus its resources? Or is it a predictable, religiously correct slogan that parrots what others in that field are already saying?

Now think about church mission statements. Most churches evangelize, make disciples, worship, create community, care for the needy, promote righteousness, and serve bad coffee. Everyone knows that not all churches are similar, yet their mission statements are fundamentally the same. Why? Because often we are unwilling to narrow the future down to the themes that are most dominant and close to our heart.

I know a church that wants to be a place where adherents can complain about how pagan and godless the church in general has become. This church wants to offer a clear alternative to today's perceived spiritual decay among Christians. However, this church's mission statement centers on the Great Commission and ministering to the world. Another church specializes in taking in those who have been rejected by angry churches, yet its mission statement is nearly identical to that of the angry church that rejects people.

Many of us refuse to create a mission statement for our life because we don't know how to do it or we fear that it's pointless. I believe we have failed to grasp the power of mission statements because we have failed to bring the notion of story into the process. My story theme must always precede my mission in the same way that who I am must be more central than what I do. Hence, a theme statement must precede a mission statement.

Theme Precedes Mission

My life story revolves around shame, violence, and arrogance; therefore my theme statement should express this thread that weaves my stories into a semicoherent tale. Here is my current theme statement: *My story reveals a surprising and unpredictable God who transforms shame through foolishness, violence through kindness, and arrogance through weakness.*

Whatever I do, however I do it, and with whomever I serve, I must live out the themes of that story. What matters most is whether we are living out the story God has written—which is the same story that he invites us to write for the future. Could I live out my mission with equal authenticity as the president of a graduate school or as an assistant pastor in an inner-city church? Yes and no. It matters what we do, but what we do matters little compared to *how* we do it.

My theme statement would make it hard for me to serve in a context where order, predictability, and formula are more valued than creativity, chaos, and complexity. My story is about shame, violence, and arrogance; therefore an environment that refused to name shame, confess violence, or expose arrogance would be like trying to hammer me, a triangular peg, into a round hole.

Also, a theme statement must move a person to say, "So what?" What difference does this statement make for the world and for a few people in it? Another person might have a very similar theme statement but a radically different mission statement. Your theme is important because it shapes your mission.

My mission involves "training truthtellers to embrace stories that transform the way we relate to others." I am an educator and a storyteller. As an educator I train people to listen and speak to the stories of the heart. But other educators who are also storytellers like me have a different life theme and mission statement. Consequently, they live out their gifts and burdens in the classroom differently than anyone else does. It is never enough to say, "I'm called to teach." Teachers must know how their story is to shape their singular way of teaching that, in turn, shapes their unique mission statement. In my calling, I most want to see hearts transformed and enabled to relate to God and to others in a fashion that is full of passion, struggle, and surrender. That personal mission shapes the dreams and goals of my life.

What I've described so far is my big story. But it is meaningless until I live into the scenes of what is immediately before me, the present story.

The Present Story: Context and People

Our mission loses breadth if we don't dream a big story, but we can't develop depth to our mission until our larger story is rooted in a real situation. If our story is not embedded in the dirt of real life, we will end up living with fantasies. And there are many who wear out their life in the safety and seclusion of couch-potato dreams. The most tragic example is the person whose dreams revolve around winning the lottery. Variants are the woman who waits for Prince Charming or the man whose career is stuck in the pathos of mediocrity but who dreams of one day gaining the corner office. Dreams can quickly become fantasies if we refuse to risk and bleed for our future.

At the same time, reality is that we are situated beings who can't extricate ourselves from our particular world by mere will. We can't will away a birth defect. We can't will away lung damage due to past smoking. We have been written by God to take up our pen and follow him, and to do so with dreams of redemption that take into account our situation.

For example, it would be foolish for me to dream of becoming president of the United States when I have never involved myself in local politics. I must take my situation into account as I write my story. It is similar to a painter who is given a small canvas to use for a painting. The painter would be foolish to use the small canvas to paint a complex battle scene. And if he is given only a few colors, then he is to use what he has to create something of beauty.

Past tragedy and pain are the paints and canvas we are to use to create the art of our life. The marks of our past form the contours that make us a creation filled with intrigue, mystery, and meaning. Why not glory in my large nose, curly hair, and piercing eyes? Oh, they have gotten me into trouble, but they've also invested me with stories that blond, blue-eyed, button-nosed boys never seem to tell.

Back to our story in our present. It has a body, space, time, and people, and we are meant to live it out while keeping in focus the horizon of our bigger story. So what do we do with our present situation? To answer that question, we need to consider what is immediately in front of us and ask ourselves three core questions:

- Do I embrace, take care of, and have gratitude for my current situation?
- Do I take responsibility for the world that has been both given to me and created by me?
- Do I bring my story and mission to bear in my present?

Let me put this bluntly: Most of us feel outnumbered and outgunned by our current situation. We want to be freed from our problems so that we can get on with our pleasures. But God has a different plan. He wants our problems to serve as the context for knowing him and living out the story he invites us to write for his glory. This means the present is not meant primarily to be resolved, or even learned from, but to be written in a way that allows us to reveal God to others and to let him reveal himself to us.

An absence of gratitude with regard to our present compels us to change it rather than be transformed by it. But with gratitude and care, we can own our present and state the obvious: what I am right now may not be all that I want to be. And if that's the case, I can begin to write a new sentence, and then a new paragraph, page, chapter. By taking ownership of all that I am and am not, I create space to write my story in light of the known past and the unseen future. It is time to write with God.

WRITING WITH GOD

At the moment I serve as the president of Mars Hill Graduate School. Initially, I didn't want to be president, and throughout my tenure I've made more mistakes than most presidents ever get the opportunity to make and still keep their jobs. I am at best a reluctant president, and our institution has suffered from the lack of a true day-to-day, buck-stops-here leader.

Why am I so reluctant to lead? In part because of my story. When my mother remarried after my birth father died in an automobile accident, she chose a man who was utterly different from my biological father. My stepfather was quiet and unassuming. He didn't take a commanding, charismatic role in the family, so decision making was up for grabs. Because I was the focus of my mother's life, my desires ruled. I recall the day my parents asked me, when I was but eight years old, if I wanted to go on a summer vacation. When I said yes, they asked where I wanted to go. I asked to see an atlas and then made the decision that we would go to California. I was too young to be in charge, and I loved the power but hated the responsibility.

Eventually I fled from that power because I refused to bear the responsibility. I can look at four decades of my life as a flight from leadership. I led, but I did so in the realm of ideas and stories, not in the world of organization and people.

So God has written me into a corner. He brilliantly inscribes our life to put us at a crossroads where we must either write with his glory to the extreme or douse the dream and refuse to imagine our future. I find it comical, or at least ironic, that I was a child who was a leader, and that I refused to lead, and that I have been thrown into leadership where I must lead, and that I have had to find a chief operating officer who can take over day-to-day leadership.

As complex as all our lives seem to be, God's plan is quite simple. He calls us to

- begin anywhere, and he will take us where he wants us to go;
- start with our strengths, and he will reveal and use our weaknesses;
- follow our desires, and he will grow his passion in us.

Granted, we may not have the slightest idea what to do about the monumental financial or physical calamity we face. It has sapped our energy and stolen our joy. What are we to do? We are to write.

The first step is to take pen and paper, or computer keyboard and screen, and write. Start by stating the obvious: *What am I up against?* Then name your desire: *What do I want to see happen?* It is wise to write out different desires related to the same calamity. Of course you want your debt or illness to go away, but once the obvious is said, what more do you really want for yourself and for the people affected by the situation? Once that is named, then you have to ask another hard question: *What do I bring to this situation for good that gives impetus to the realization of my dreams, and what do I bring that impedes the realization of my dreams?*

All of this writing serves as prelude to the hardest question of all: *What do I want to become, and what do I want to reveal about God through this process?* In the midst of writing the present, you must draw from the past in order to imagine the future.

In my life, the process of facing why I don't want to lead on a day-to-day basis has revealed much of my past that I didn't want to face. But in embracing my story with gratitude, honoring my present responsibility, and risking for what lies ahead, I have clearly seen that I am not to write myself into a life of day-to-day administrative decision making.

Finally, know that the writing process can't be done in isolation from others who are writing their lives. We are meant to write in community. We are meant to turn our first draft (and second, third, and fourth) over to good editors, to our good friends who have eyes not only for our present but also for the larger story we are written to tell. It is through cowriting not only with God but also with our communities that we come to write with greater depth and breadth. So we now turn to the task of writing and editing with others.

Telling Your Story

As you write the stories of your life, you go deeper into scenes of pain and loss. "Coming to love your own life requires you to believe that the past is God's will...ultimately written for both his glory and your participation in his redemption.... He uses pain and brokenness, just as he uses shalom." With that in mind, what would you like to offer to those who suffer in the same ways you have suffered?

chapter eight

editing together

Allowing Others to Ask the "So What?" Question

Almost all good writing begins with terrible
first efforts. You need to start somewhere, so
start by getting something—anything—down
on paper. One friend says the first draft is the
down draft—you get it down. The second
draft is the up draft—you fix it up. You try to
say what you have to say more accurately. And
the third draft is the dental draft, where you
check every tooth to see if it's loose or cramped
or decayed or even, God help us, healthy.

ANNE LAMOTT

A friend of mine read the first seven chapters of this book and remarked, "Do you actually think I'm going to write?" I was baffled. Our conversation turned to his resistance to write a single word about his life. He said, "I enjoyed the book as long as I thought you were using the word *write* as a metaphor. But when it became clear you wanted me to actually write things down, I thought, *Forget it.*"

This man is a capable professional, bright and successful. He writes reports and client summaries every day. But for some reason, the moment he thought about writing about his life, he froze. He's not alone. The excuses for not writing are legion: "I can't spell, my grammar is atrocious, I get bored, what's the point, someone might read it, I don't have time, it seems so self-indulgent, my stories are painful, I feel too much when I write." The struggle is somewhat similar to praying, fasting, or giving away our goods: because we don't do it well, we choose not to do anything at all. We have an image of good or even perfect writing (or praying, fasting, giving), and since we can't achieve what we idealize, then it's just easier not to risk.

My friend's reasons boiled down to these: frustration, futility, and fear. His frustration centered on the few times that he had written from his heart and discovered that he couldn't say what he felt. Each time he wrote, his words seemed flat and hollow compared to what he was experiencing. Writing is always a form of translation. We take what is in us and bring it up from our heart through our mind to the page. That translation always leaves much unsaid. The labor to say it again—better—is agonizing. Many quit before the depth of their story rises in the words.

My friend's frustration led to a feeling of futility. He said bluntly, "Why should I do something that is so hard and so guaranteed to fail?" The failure is not only in not saying something that is in accord with one's heart, but it also involves the futility of "So what?" Once I've written something about my life—so what? What am I to do with a new understanding of how hard it was to make the transition to the new school in fifth grade or how painful it was to be humiliated in junior-high gym class? Those tough periods in life are, thankfully, over. And the tough periods in life right now need action, not writing, to resolve. Writing feels pointless.

It's difficult to respond to such questions. But my friend is a good athlete who works out regularly, so I compared writing to running. It seldom feels fantastic to run, but each day even a short run builds strength that is cumulative and energizes the body and mind to better tackle the demands of the day. Writing, even a few sentences or a few words, brings us face to face with our present life and calls us to engage in truths that are otherwise too easy to ignore. Then my friend admitted his reluctance really had far more to do with fear.

None of us wants to dredge up the past—especially the hurt and tragedy and abuse we find there. And writing a sentence makes that reality of life harder to escape. My friend admitted that when he wrote even a few sentences about matters in his past, everything became more real. There is something about seeing your hurts and struggles in black and white that focuses the heart rather than allowing it to turn and flee. We are more naked and needy before words that we write than perhaps anywhere else. We fear this, so we avoid it.

But reality is where God shows up. Reality may be painful, but if we want to meet God we have to go there. Writing is a fearful and wonderful gift we give to God, an offering of sacrifice given in hope of redemption.

We can write for hours or seconds. We can write a diary, journal, scenes, dreams, plans, essays, poetry, mission statements, lists, and letters to a deceased abuser, friend, parent, or God. The world changes the moment we write a sentence, because we can't write just one. One sentence, one honest series of words, whether grammatically correct or spelled well, calls forth its twin. Two sentences ache for a third. If you write three sentences, you will inevitably write more. And once you are writing, you find that the kind of writing destined to tell the truth and direct your life must eventually be read by an editor.

O Trusted Editor

We must submit our story, the writing of our life, to the reading of others. And we must do so with people we deeply trust. Otherwise the naked experience of baring our stories to another will bring shame and send us fleeing.

A few years ago I wrote a book called *How Children Raise Parents.* The first time I read portions of that manuscript to a group, I found it far more difficult than I imagined. I felt exposed and vulnerable. I wondered how people would receive my words, and I found it nearly impossible to raise my eyes as I read. I was afraid to look at the group's expression.

The experience is not a great deal different when a friend quietly reads, in my presence, something I've written. As I see his or her pen circle a word or cross out a clause or write a remark in the margin, I can't help but interrupt: "So what do you think?" It's humbling to invite another person to see and respond to your creation, and it is utterly imperative to do so if we want to know the truth about our story.

My books have had the enormous care and generosity of editors who bring tears to my heart when I think about how they attended their labor. Each book has one professional editor assigned, but I've also been blessed to have many friends who read each chapter even before it lands on the editor's desk. These friends served as attendants to the birth, and each brought a lifetime of care to the process.

A good editor, and any good reader of the early drafts, is a midwife. S/he is both tender enough not to shame the groaning or despise the blood and strong enough to demand concentrated focus to push through the pain at the right season. A dear friend who reads and asks good, hard questions invites us to dig deeper, see the horizon, and press on to answer the question, "So what?"

Digging Deeper

If we write a diary or a journal, seldom is there a need for a rewrite. That kind of writing underscores the rhythms of the day and of our inner world, and it is fodder for other kinds of writing. But when we write a scene from our life or we work on naming the themes of our story or we focus on a mission statement, then it is imperative that we write, rewrite, and rewrite the rewrite. Rewriting digs deeper into the soil of our story.

That digging is important because all writing leaves gaps. These gaps hold a depth that can be explored only after repeated encounters. But entering into our story gaps requires an outside reading by a good editor who opens the text to a new reading. The new reading can give us a perspective that we did not see before.

Judi, a student at Mars Hill Graduate School, met with me for a twenty-minute office appointment. We had a lovely conversation, but she was so earnest and worked so hard to make sure each word was clear and well chosen that after five minutes I felt exhausted for her. I asked at one point, "Have you ever talked with anyone where you could relax and be young?" She seemed startled, but she regained her composure in the blink of an eye.

I pressed just a little harder. "I suspect you've always been the most

responsible and diligent person in your family. You don't seem to rest well."
She didn't speak; she nodded her head. I asked, "What would it be like if,
during your time with us at Mars Hill, you experimented with letting others be more responsible than you are? What would it be like to play, not
earn straight As, not be the first to answer a question, and perhaps even to
mess up in ways you've never permitted yourself to in the past?"

I talked with Judi a few months later. She told me that when we first
spoke, I might as well have counseled her to abuse drugs, dye her hair pink,
and work for the Communist Party. She was highly offended, and it took
several weeks to name that something had stung her far beyond what she
felt was my inaccurate reading of her life. But she began to look at her life
in a new light. She was the oldest child in the family, and at a young age
she realized her mother was flighty and dishonest. Her mother might tell a
pointless lie or take a loaf of bread from the grocery store without paying
for it. She might start reading a book and forget to prepare dinner for the
family.

Judi was her mother's safety net and her siblings' functioning parent. It
wasn't a surprise that by age twenty-four Judi had already known success as
a youth pastor, camp counselor, church secretary, and salesperson. She had
already been picked to be the next women's ministry coordinator at her
home church. Her calling seemed settled and clear.

But my reading of her life, as well as my editorial questions and remarks,
cast her into a quandary. She found herself asking, *Is this really my calling,
or is it merely an opportunity to repeat the patterns of the past by being the most
responsible person around?* Judi's story is still evolving, but she has begun to
write new paragraphs about what she wants to become rather than merely
following the groove of a familiar, well-worn rut. She may end up being a

women's ministry coordinator, or she may end up writing a brand-new story for her life.

Judi had invited me to read her life and enter her story to ponder its gaps and inconsistencies, the things that make little sense. She asked me to be an editor. A good editor draws out what is not said in order to give life to what was aborted before it saw the light of day. We need friends who will name what is unnamed in our story, so that the truth is told. A good editor also helps to ensure that we don't edit out the truth. And a good editor helps us consider the implications of what our story tells us about ourselves.

Seeing the Horizon

A good friend is an editor who walks around our story in widening circles and at different heights to help us see not only where we have come from but also where we might go. Editing takes us to our mission through the meaning of our story.

For sixteen years I've been part of leading a week of reflection and recovery for men and women who have been sexually abused. It has been one of the greatest privileges of my life to see men and women face their histories of torment and join with others in grieving and raging against the darkness. These times have been profoundly transforming for everyone. Many of those who went through the one-week course asked if there could be a second week. This time, since I was in the midst of reflecting on story and the power of writing, I agreed.

The dilemma was that now I would need to write about the abuse in my own history, just as I had asked the participants to do with their lives. I had written before about being abused, but I had never written anything about the abuse itself. As I began to write, I experienced flashbacks, nausea, rage, and profound fear. I even questioned whether the abuse had ever actually happened.

To follow is the scene that I wrote that week.

Nine Weeks

The cabin was no more than three hundred square feet with two bunk beds on the sides and two desks at the back of the plank-floored space. We were in West Virginia, it was mid-June, and the windows were all mesh screens to keep out the mosquitoes. There were at least eight cabins on each side. One row backed up to the river, and the other was twenty yards set back from the river row. The arrangement of cabins seemed to follow the plan of army barracks. The flagpole was at the head of the encampment, and I could hear the cloth stiffen and flutter late at night as the hot winds blew through our screens. The sound reminded me that tomorrow morning, no matter what happened in the dark, another day would rise, and we would all stand at attention and bark out the Pledge of Allegiance.

It was always my hope that the morning would come and I'd have slept through the night, not being awakened by the creaking of the old springs in a bed or the low moan of breath quickening until it escaped in a final rush of fury.

But night scared me for another reason. It was when the counselors told stories of past campers. It often began with the chiding and supercilious warnings not to leave the cabin after hours. No one was stupid enough to venture outside after lights off. Night after night we heard the same story, in different forms, about campers who had ventured off to slide down the embankment to the river and were never found. One or two variations were told that included bodies, mauled by some wild predator, bloated and pus-filled, floating down the river. It was enough to recall the horror of Jim and Huck coming upon the corpse in the rotted old boat, but when I considered that this could be *my* body that was discovered, I knew I would not only not leave the cabin, but I'd do whatever I was told so I could avoid such a fate.

I was a pudgy, kinky-haired, pimply, young eleven-year-old. I had discovered my penis only four months earlier during a camping trip when my scoutmaster had asked me to touch his erect member. It was as if I had awakened at that moment to a world that seemed to be phallic in plain view of everyone. I began to hear what I had never been aware of before—sexual humor, innuendos, taunts, and invitations. It was as if the world had been speaking a language I had never heard until that moment. Through this act of "initiation," I was not only given the ears to hear but also a mouth that could speak. I was startled and repulsed, aroused and intrigued.

Before I left home for the camp in West Virginia, my dad had said, "Don't tell your mom that you'll be staying at camp nine weeks. Once you get there, call us and beg us to let you stay, and I'll make it happen." I knew he was afraid of my mom, but I had never realized he was so manipulative. I just played along.

Once I arrived at the camp, I made the phone call. The die was cast, and soon afterward I experienced my first moment of torture. Late at night the boys in my cabin were forced to exit our beds and undress in front of the counselors. Our bodies were prodded and exposed by the riding crops the counselors used to make the camp's horses run with more gusto. Now the same leather devices were used to humiliate and dehumanize us. We were to stand motionless, silent, and seemingly unaware of what was happening to the camper standing next to us.

Then we were told to start running. A mass of naked boys silhouetted by a broken moon took off for the baseball fields. I was near the front because our cabin was second from the top, but within a short distance, the strong legs and thin bodies of my peers outran me, and I was soon near the back of the group. One of the counselors had taken off his whistle so he could whip me with the strap as he laughed at my slow pace. I ran as hard as I could. I could feel my loose tummy rock to and fro, and no matter how hard I willed or wished, I could not outrun my tormentor. The more he whipped, the harder I ran and the slower I became. The wind in my lungs heaved and became heavier, and my legs churned as I raced away from the pain, but what stung more than the stripes on my buttocks was the pure delight in his laughter. He howled and cooed with amusement. I hated him. I hated his cackle and his pagan pleasure. I hated his southern drawl and his piercing blue eyes. He became my most consistent and gleeful tormentor. He loved to grab my sprawling flesh in his hand and squeeze. He promised me that I would leave his camp thin and mean. And he was a man of his word. He squeezed me dry for nine, long, lonely, fearful weeks.

♦

I wrote that scene for the first time in my life. The men and women from the sexual-abuse recovery group who had stayed for a second week read and heard my words. One person wept and another couldn't look at me. The conversation was intense and rich, and the questions that arose prompted me to begin to make connections I had not considered when I wrote the first draft. One person asked about my loss of innocence when I faced my father's manipulation. Another asked if I had noticed the contempt I seemed to have for that young boy's body. As the conversation continued, the group encouraged me to enter the terror that seemed to be laced with shame.

As leader of the group, I felt it important to submit my writing to others, but I had not expected such strong emotion as I read nor the new data that arose in the conversation. I had always thought of my stepfather as a quiet and passive man but never as manipulative. Even my own writing didn't convince me. I had written it, but the words violated my image of my father. He may have been manipulative in that one scene, but he wasn't a manipulative man. The group asked me, "What do you have to give up if your image of your father changes?" As I pursued that question with a single sentence, and then a paragraph, and eventually many paragraphs, it opened my heart to new levels of being orphaned and of God hearing the cries of an orphan.

My editors were inviting me to dig deeper and look at the broader implications of my story. They dug deep with me to unearth my father's manipulation, but I didn't want to see it as true. They went further and asked me to look at the horizon and name what it would cost me to take this journey to truth. When they asked me to name the cost, I was compelled to face a simple truth: my father used me to soothe and calm my mother when she was sad and upset. He confided in me, and I was his secret-bearer who helped keep the marriage intact and alive. He betrayed me. He set me up to keep secrets, which I had done so very well even with regard to the abuse. I thought I had broken the silence and named the abuse by speaking and writing about it. I had, but I did not enter all the implications of the harm until I put the words on a page.

A good editor will ask the horizon question: where is this journey taking you? And the answer is always beyond what we can see. It is the same with words. We can never fully say all that is inside us. The more important it is, the more we stammer. But an editor presses us to peer beyond what we've said to where the words take us. An editor calls us to press harder and push beyond the agony of unbirthed words so that they can be spoken.

Facing my father's manipulative betrayal helped me name a series of betrayals at the hands of older men, mentors, and leaders. What surprised me in the grief was the care of my Creator Father. He was neither surprised by nor afraid of my fury; nor did he allow me to ignore the story he had written in me through those losses. His kindness softened my heart and enabled me to begin to name the many times I had betrayed others just as I had been betrayed. Even in the deeper grief of my sin, God was neither surprised nor afraid of my shame. His presence, his strong embrace, melted away some of the glacial coldness in my heart.

Yes, a good editor calls you to the horizon where God has been waiting to receive you as you journey back to his presence. It is this attraction of home that allows an editor to ask one of the hardest questions: "So what?"

Pressing On to "So What?"

No doubt you've listened to someone tell a long, tiresome story, and you had to wonder, "When will this ever end?" Likewise, it's possible to listen to a great story and still wonder, "What's the point?" Both questions are really asking, "So what?" Whether the story is well told and interesting or more tedious than watching grass grow, we inevitably want to know the point: what am I to do with what I've just heard?

Seldom will a piece of writing translate into an immediate, concrete action. Perhaps reading a good stock tip might cause a person to go online and within minutes purchase the stock. But reading a poem, for instance, seldom rallies a reader to take immediate action.

More likely, a poem, novel, or magazine article is read and enjoyed as a pleasant way to pass the time. It may add a few tidbits of information to our vast storehouse of facts before being promptly forgotten. What if we asked the question, "So what?" during and after every television show and movie and poem and novel? My guess is that we wouldn't waste as much time in the drivel of mere entertainment.

By asking, "So what?" I enter the realm of meaning and creativity, and I am no longer a consumer. The question compels me to create and author my life in light of my own reading of the text. Imagine reading a poem, let alone writing one, and then asking these questions: *What am I to become? If I am moved by something I've written or read, then what is it in my life that rose up in response? What is it about the way I live out my marriage, my friendships, or my job that was stirred by what I read or wrote? And if the reading or the writing failed to touch me, then what's missing? How do I get to the stories that transform my life?* Good friends are editors who read our writing and hear our stories with an ear to answer the question underlying all these other questions: "So what?"

As our reality is named, we are moved to ponder the implications of our story, but we can't stop there. We must also ask and be asked: What will you do with what you've written? If it moves you, will you move? And if you move, where will you go, what are the risks, and how will you know when you've arrived? Most of us don't invite a community of friends to know our story deeply enough to meaningfully engage the question, "So what?" The result is that our story, often our life, fails to move with integrity toward transformation. We will never change unless we risk action. We will never change unless we act in accord with the trajectory of our story. And friends who are good editors invite us to take that risk.

While there is much to be seen in our story and much to be removed, depth is not the only concern. A good editor is also looking to expand our story, to broaden our worldview. We need editing that helps us see the terrain on which we walk. Again, it is a matter of focus. I can look so closely at the details of my story that I forget about obtaining a more expansive view of my life.

Clearly an editor undertakes a paradoxical task. S/he helps you see the point of your story, but without becoming fixed on it. A good editor reminds the writer to press on to the end without becoming bound to what that end will be. There may be a sense of where a work is going, but there are so many twists and turns in the process that the end must be honored and allowed to occur without our foreknowledge or interference. This calls us to persevering, relentless openness. It is where we must be as stubborn as a mule to wait for the story to be completed. And as we wait, it's good to remember that all endings are the sweet gift of a new beginning. Even the ending of this earth is but the beginning of the rest of eternity.

Yet an editor moves us to a temporary, incomplete ending. As relentless as we must be to leave the ending unattended, we must also unreservedly move toward an ending. We can't write forever. We must eventually risk by acting. And our risk is a solitary act. No friend, spouse, or comrade can walk with us in the risk of acting. Yes, God is with us, but his presence never takes away the necessity of risk and faith.

The paradox is that as I write alone, I write for others.

WRITING IN COMMUNITY

I am solely responsible for reading and writing my story well, for digging deep into the gaps, for finding the desire and passion and themes that God has written in my life. At the same time, I can't write alone. I am in community. For good and for ill, my story spills over to the lives of others.

Even though our story spills into the lives of others, and even though everyone is fully involved in my becoming who I am, I can blame no one for my story. Is this a contradiction? I don't think so. The reason it is not contradictory is simple: I will be the only person who stands before the face of God to take account for my life. Many have influenced me—both for good and ill—but I will not be able to bring a small group before the throne of God and say, "They are the ones who made me this way." We live as one, but it is always a one formed by many. The pleasure of being a community of stories on this side of heaven is to mimic, poorly and incompletely, the day in which we will feast together on the stories of God.

Let's turn now to a story feast.

Telling Your Story

Your stories are not meant for you alone but for others as well. We write our stories and edit them in relationship with others. With that in mind, think about where and to whom you tell your most painful and vulnerable stories.

multiplying your story

chapter nine

story feasting

The Community That Helps Rewrite Your Story

Being free means "being free for the other,"
because the other has bound me to him.
Only in relationship with the other am I free.
DIETRICH BONHOEFFER

Reading and writing our story becomes a lonely affair if it's done outside of community. Stories are meant to be told, heard, and retold with others. I have worked with Kirk and Heather Webb at Mars Hill Graduate School for a decade, and I know many of their stories by heart. Recently, as we had dinner with some adjunct faculty, I begged Kirk to tell a few of his infamous stories.

As he told a story about trying to get a date as an eighth grader, I dined on the exquisite interplay of shame, pathos, humor, and glory wedded into his masterful storytelling. It wasn't just the story that thrilled me; it was the rich humanity he called forth as we all recalled some of our worst dating memories from that fragile season of life.

We laughed until we cried. It is a funny, awful story, and it brought to light other realities of our lives. Every one of us is also an awkward teenager trying to look cool, but in fact we're making fools of ourselves.

Stories are food for friends to feast on together. We are called to write and then rewrite, and we also are called to tell our stories to people who love us, people who will celebrate our life. We need people who will ponder our stories and help us write with more integrity and depth. But we need more than mere feedback; we need celebration.

I need my friends to laugh and also to weep with me. I will never write the story that reveals my name, let alone transforms my name, unless I am in a community where we love, celebrate, and feast in the midst of our shared stories.

A Story Encounter

I met Elizabeth in Pensacola, Florida. My friend Tremper and I had been invited to speak at the prestigious Pensacola Theological Institute. Through the decades, this annual conference had sponsored some of the luminaries—and I mean the brightest stars—of the conservative Presbyterian and Reformed camp. I had no idea why they had sunk so low as to invite me, but once I knew the invitation was not a hoax, I agreed to go.

Tremper and I arrived at the Bible conference, and the evening meal was served outdoors. Often the speakers at such an event are given a wide berth, so Tremper and I ate alone until one couple joined us.

The suffocating heat of Pensacola was a stark contrast to our conversations with Elizabeth and her husband, Kip. Elizabeth was a generous southern hostess who laced our evening conversations with saucy questions about the Old Testament and various matters of the heart. Mealtime with Kip and Elizabeth became our most anticipated time of the day. We had numerous discussions about their lives and ours. We covered history, heartache, redemption, and hope. In a short season, we became friends.

Little did I know that Elizabeth is a gifted writer and an enormous risk-taker. She took some of the material that Tremper and I taught at the conference and produced a study guide that she used in the lives of the women who attend Moms' Group at her home church. With these women, she then began to have intermittent story feasts where women could share what was happening in their lives, read their writing, and invite others to celebrate or sorrow over the current glory (or plight) of their narrative.

In order to write and then really hear the meaning of our story, we must be in community. To be empowered and encouraged to keep writing, reading, and editing, we must be with other hearts that feast over our story. With this in mind, I've asked Elizabeth to tell her story and also the story of Moms' Group and its story feasts.

ELIZABETH'S STORY OF STORIES

What, you may be asking, am I doing in the middle of Dan Allender's book? I suppose it's because I'm an ordinary mother of four with a passion for telling and hearing stories. You might object to what Dan has asked you to do in previous chapters. After all, he inhabits a world where people actually enjoy laboring over their stories and then reading them to one another. But before you shy away from writing your own story the way Dan invites you to, first read about the Lord working in and through the stories of ordinary women in a moms' group in a church in Florida.

The Story of Moms' Group

I was running on a treadmill, heavily pregnant with my third child. I do my best creative work in the last month of pregnancy, and this time I began to conceive of a group for moms. Having two children already, I deeply doubted my calling to motherhood. Now, pregnant with my third, I was beginning to panic. I wanted help. My vision was that some of the moms with older kids (and more kids) would speak to some of us younger moms on practical issues of child-raising. It would be a short series of seminars, say four to six weeks.

I discussed the idea with our pastor's wife, and before I knew it, a group of moms was meeting weekly to watch a video series. At first the pastor's wife and I were coleaders, but she soon moved on to other duties and I became the leader, a calling that prompted me to deeply doubt God's wisdom. But I carried forth, leading by humiliation, figuring that my best bet was to be honest about my numerous flaws as a mother.

That was in 1993, and Moms' Group has evolved since then. We've tried new things and deepened relationships in a variety of ways—including the launch of Story Feasts. The story of Story Feasts begins in August 1996 when Dan Allender and Tremper Longman III landed in Pensacola, Florida, for a week of Bible conference lectures. The topic was "Worship and the Heart," and I had never heard of the speakers. But since I then had four children aged six and younger, I was determined to plant them in the conference's "Junior Institute" while I sat in the air-conditioned sanctuary and caught up on my sleep.

The great Author of story had a different idea. I arrived late to Dan's Tuesday-morning lecture. Having glanced at the title, "Idolatry and Self-Worship," I plopped down and prepared to get some rest. After all, I didn't have any graven images sitting around my house. Then Dan told a story that pierced my heart—he told of escaping to a library after a humiliating experience. He asked the question: "Where do you go in moments of shame to find security and significance?" Unfortunately, I have a great love for libraries. I'd been caught, and I did something I'd never done in church before. I began to weep. Books were always my safety zone when my chaotic world began to fall in on me. I had not realized something so precious could become a false god.

As the week went on, Dan and Tremper double-teamed me with words of awakening that God wished me to hear. On Wednesday night, as the two partners in crime sat sweating it out over fried fish, I marched up and asked them to leave. Actually, I just suggested that they take the following day off, and I offered to take them windsurfing or scuba diving or fishing. (I'd do anything to get the Holy Spirit off my back.) I will never forget the looks on their faces—Tremper's alarm and Dan's amusement—which rushed me to the concluding sentence of my speech: "You've done way too much good around here."

They had propelled me toward story in a way I had never known possible. From an early age, I had turned to books as a retreat from chaos; I had found the storied words soothing in a world where spoken words carried with them violence and abandonment. I had filled pages and pages of spiral notebooks with the stories of my life, mostly recorded like Harlequin romances. From my youngest days, I knew in my gut that story was important, but now my eyes were opening to the fact that my story was not a random series of events, but one that contained pattern and purpose, some of it unpalatable.

God had written Dan and Tremper into my story during a hot Florida summer in order to rekindle in me a burning fire for God's story, his Word, as well as to open my eyes to the words that lay buried in my suffocating heart.

In the following months and years, I began to rewrite my story. My original version was a chirpy, Christianized variant of my parents' telling. It went like this: "Yeah, it was kinda bad growing up in a home of divorce. But God was good to me and provided so many teachers and adult friends who provided me nurture and showed me his love." That was nothing more than a sweet fantasy. The reality was that the split, which occurred when I was seven, left me orphaned, widowed, and exiled—all in the short time it took my mother to drive my brother and me the sixty miles from Carrollton, Georgia, to Atlanta.

As I began to read and rewrite my story, I discovered that in the divorce I had lost not only my mother and father but also my name, my words, and my voice. I acknowledged for the first time that some of the adults who had moved into my life to nurture and mentor me were male teachers who abused their power and position in order to bind my soul to theirs in wicked ways. They had linked my love for words to their erotic intentions. And then, in an odd twist, the name they had assigned me, A Dangerous Woman, stuck in my soul. The result was many years of not using my voice or embracing the sensual joy of words. Slowly, I found my voice, retrieved my words, and began to recognize my name. Indeed, that name is Dangerous, but not in the way those men intended.

As I began to name the truth about my story, I realized that others might be offering sham versions of their stories as well. A passion and call-ing that had been a driving theme of my life took shape: to help people—but in particular the orphan, the widow, and the stranger—recover their lost words, return to despised stories, and read them for the first time. The women of Moms' Group started doing this in community, where each of us was invited to celebrate God's handwriting on our soul.

The First Story Feast

The first time I went to Moms' Group with the idea of doing a Story Feast, I had the naive expectation that everyone would be as thrilled as I was about telling her story. It seemed to me a simple assignment. I asked them to write and tell a story of rescue, and I explained that they'd have two weeks to come up with one. When I handed out the instructions, their uncomprehending, dismayed expressions told me that not everyone be-lieved telling their story would be such fun. Still, on the day of the feast, ten women arrived with good food and wild stories.

Why a feast? Because feasting is a lost art in a culture where the average family meal lasts just twelve minutes. Yet feasting is a key theme of the Bible. God's people gathered at appointed times to reflect on his rescue in their lives. Passover, one of Israel's most important feasts, was followed by the Feast of Unleavened Bread. These two feasts together recalled God's rescue of his people from Egypt and his provision for them during their journey. Participants included everyone in the community, men and women, young and old, orphan, stranger, and widow. The feast revolved around ritual food (meat, bread, and wine), which was offered and eaten as a sacrifice to God.

But why must we, as Christians, feast together on story? Because the stories of redemption involve the sweat and earth of sorrow and the tanta-lizing aroma of freshly baked provision. Feasting involves nourishing our bodies with both story and food. So many Bible studies are dull and pro-saic—the antithesis of redemption. We get together and treat the Bible as a textbook, and then, almost bored to a comfortable slumber, we liven things up by telling juicy gossip, also known as prayer requests. We should breathe a collective groan of repentance.

There's an even more important reason for feasting. The Christian tra-dition takes the Old Testament sacrament of feasting to a new and bizarre level when Christ says, "I assure you, unless you eat the flesh of the Son of Man and drink his blood, you cannot have eternal life within you. But those who eat my flesh and drink my blood have eternal life, and I will raise them at the last day."[1] (I always think that if Dan was troubled years ago by a preacher mentioning a "talking ass," it's a very good thing his first exposure to Christian sermons didn't introduce him to this apparently cannibalistic statement.) Indeed, as we celebrate the sacrament of Holy Communion, we are feasting on Christ's body and blood, doing this in remembrance of the greatest story of rescue ever known. But as we follow Christ, we must do more than feast on him. We must gather together and offer our own stories as the bread and wine that sustain the life of the com-munity. In so doing, we celebrate the faith, hope, and love that mark us as Christians.

FEASTING ON THREE QUESTIONS

Key to our Story Feast is this passage: "Now the angel of the LORD found her by a spring of water in the wilderness.... He said, 'Hagar, Sarai's maid, where have you come from and where are you going?'"[2] At its most basic level, a story feast brings our community together to address the three ques-tions—two stated, one implied—that we find in the angel's words:

- Where have you been? (the past)
- Where are you now? (the present)
- Where are you going? (the future)

To address these questions in community is to begin the process of editing our story. In that process, we begin to see the unseen, name the unnamed, and dream the impossible. With new insight provided by those who love us, we are prepared to begin rewriting our story to the glory of our Author.

Where Have You Been?

The Angel of the Lord approached Hagar, who, harassed by her mistress, had fled to the desert, and invited her to tell her story. The first element of a story feast is such an invitation to story. And so Moms' Group breaks from regular book study about every six weeks to invite stories related to the themes we are studying. In the summer, we meet every other week to tell stories around a given theme. Here are a few story topics:

Out of the Mouths of Babes. The Bible tells us that God disciplines those he loves.[3] Hebrews 12, the Bible's most famous chapter on discipline, tells us it's a privilege to be disciplined by God. But have you ever thought the Lord might use your children to discipline you, to teach you? At a story feast, tell about a time when God used one of your children to show you something about yourself, about himself, or about the world. Even if you don't have children, you may have been taught by someone else's child. If not, tell of a time that you as a child taught one of your parents something.

Creatively Recalling. Zakar is one word used for story in the Bible; the definition of *zakar* teaches that stories incorporate the concepts of recollection and remembrance. The biblical reference point for this story topic is the stones of remembrance mentioned in the book of Joshua.[4] In Joshua 4, God commanded the Israelites to collect stones from the riverbed. Joshua explained, "We will use these stones to build a memorial. In the future, your children will ask, 'What do these stones mean to you?' Then you can tell them, 'They remind us that the Jordan River stopped flowing when the Ark of the LORD's covenant went across.'"[5] At a story feast, share stories that stand for you as a permanent memorial to God's goodness, provision, or rescue in your life. What memories do you have of God's working in your life in a powerful way?

Death of a Vision or Dream. This topic is inspired by the story of David, who dreamed of building a temple for the Lord.[6] Then God told him that another king would undertake that task. David was devastated, but he took his deep disappointment and turned it into praise. At a story feast, tell about a time you had a dream or a vision, and it died. Did God open another door, or did God later fulfill your vision (or dream) in an unexpected way? Or tell about a dream fulfilled and how God fulfilled it!

In Moms' Group over the years, I've heard funny stories and tragic stories; stories of worship, war, and waiting; stories of school, summer, and stumbling. As we gather over good food, believing that the richness of the fare is a small taste of the coming banquet in heaven, I usually lead off with a short introduction to the theme we're discussing. Then someone tells a story, and the feasting begins in earnest. We laugh until we cry, we cry until we laugh, we ask questions to clarify. Sometimes we prod and poke the story and its teller; other times we simply offer the silence and space that the story requires. The preparation for the feast begins with recalling and writing the stories; the feast itself gives opportunity for reading and editing. After the feast may come a fast where we pray, grieve, and rewrite.

To give you a clearer picture of what this looks like, here is an example of Moms' Group members telling, editing, and rewriting their stories. Or more accurately, it's an example of the rewriting of souls that occurs during a story feast.

At a feast last summer, "Death of a Vision," I told a story about my struggle in a class I took at Mars Hill Graduate School in Seattle. The moms responded with brilliant and kind editing that gave me the courage to rewrite and recognize where the heart of the battle lay. Here is the skeletal version of the story I told:

This summer I took a class at MHGS that made me deeply question my dream of finishing my degree, a pursuit that was foolish at best, impossible at worst. I had already taken six classes at Mars Hill, and each had changed my heart in profound ways. I had always left Mars with a renewed passion for God, my calling, and my community. But this class made me feel crazy. The atmosphere felt cynical and mocking, and my body was tied in tense knots as I sat through the seven hours of class for four days in a row. Before this experience I had always looked forward to "flying out to Mars" for a week; I had the sense that this extraterrestrial world was indeed my home.

But during this week of class, I began to feel like an alien in a land where I had previously thought my language was spoken. My world was unmade, and I was hurled into doubt, despair, and pain. The professor of the class seemed to earmark me for ambiguous and provocative interactions. I found that I doubted my instincts and turned against my words, alternately assuming I was stupid and then blaming anyone who didn't seem to see my viewpoint. Most of all, I felt dangerous.

After the moms heard my story, with far more detail and much more emotion than the preceding pared-down version provides, their editorial questions began. As I struggled to answer their questions, I uncovered my truer story.

First, Christie offered wisdom that moms with school-age kids know only too well: "Elizabeth, we tell our kids that some years they may get along better with their teachers than others. Anyone who's done as much school as you have has had tough encounters with professors. It sounds like this prof misused his power, but you can't let that stop you. I'm not sure God wants you to give up so quickly."

Another mom who has heard other parts of my story observed, "Yeah, and it sounds like you did something you never would have done before. You spoke up. Maybe you weren't heard by the professor. But are you going to hate yourself for that?"

With their comments and questions, these friends pointed me back to "where I had been," leading me to the story I hadn't told, a despised story that the Spirit wanted me to embrace.

The Uncovered Story

We need to remember that the themes and burdens of our life develop from our woundedness, so when we tell our stories in community, others will ask questions that help us recover our untold story. I mentioned already that in high school certain male teachers had named me A Dangerous Woman. I omitted the detail that these men were English teachers. I also omitted the detail that my father was a college English professor. Finally, I neglected to mention that I became an English teacher myself. My feasting friends pointed me toward this history, and I began to recognize that my Author had written in me a story in which a woundedness of words and body led to my passion for loosening tongues—for helping orphans, widows, and strangers find their lost voice.

From my father I first learned that words can be powerful tools of seduction. He was a brilliant English professor who labored for hours over lecture notes on William Shakespeare, John Donne, and Matthew Arnold. He was eloquent, erudite, and coolly charming. As early as I can recall, he had a flock of female followers who compared him to the likes of John Wayne and Paul Newman. In that world I first experienced the interplay of words, power, and eroticism. It was a dark lesson that was to become a theme of my academic career.

My father was my first editor. As a seven-year-old, I wrote letters home from my grandmother's house, where my brother and I spent the summer months after my parents' divorce. My father would return the letters with comma splices circled and sentence fragments marked. It was a secret joke we shared, but internally I longed to write a letter that would restore my father to my orphaned soul. My desire to write something that would please my father continued well into young adulthood. I often submitted my papers for his approval before turning them in to my professors. His critiques always left me with the awareness that my words had failed to win back my father.

It wasn't until I reached my early thirties that I began to suspect that "something [was] rotten in the state of Denmark." I was discussing my fear and hatred of writing with a friend, and I told him of a comment I had found on one of my graduate-school rough drafts. Etched in my father's art-deco handwriting was *Gross intrusion of an egregiously personal anecdote.* My friend gasped. "In writing those words," he said, "your father took away what is most lovely about your writing—your willingness to share your heart."

Many other conversations and much pondering led me to see that my father, a fearful man who would rather perish than publish, had used his power over my heart to stifle what was best about my voice. A man who used words primarily as a tool for seducing hearts to darkness had missed what I knew innately—that words are a God-given gift to compel souls to life.

It is hardly surprising that I replayed the scenario that had failed to win back my father. I searched for others, for a sort of substitute father, and I used words to try to win them. Two high-school English teachers enjoyed playing confidant and companion to me in the lonely after-school hours while I waited for my mom to pick me up. A teenage girl with no boyfriends and few dates, I poured out my ache to these men who didn't know how to honor my story. Both eventually used the power I had invested in them to feed their own fantasy lives.

One of them silenced my voice in a searing moment of high-school shame. One spring day he ambled into a musty classroom in the aged prep school carrying a stack of papers with a magazine on top. He walked behind where I was sitting with my friends at a long oak library table. Then he dropped the now-famous issue of *Time* magazine featuring supermodel Cheryl Tiegs. His lips curved mockingly as he spoke in his cool, refined voice: "Has anyone ever told you that you look like Cheryl Tiegs?" Some girls giggled; some girls glared. I stared at the picture lying on the table in front of me.

The cover of that issue of *Time* had focused on Cheryl Tiegs's gorgeous face, featuring her trademark gleaming smile. But my teacher had not shown me the magazine's cover. He had folded the magazine so that it opened to the page where Tiegs was shown in the risqué fishnet bathing suit she had modeled for a *Sports Illustrated* swimsuit issue.

I sat perfectly still, staring at this picture of a woman's body that bore no resemblance to mine. I had given this man my words and my heart in my ongoing search for a father; apparently he had used them to groom me for his perverted imagination. In this moment, I became tongue-tied.

The following year, the pattern was repeated. This time I unwittingly landed in danger on a late Friday afternoon. I was in the faculty lounge hashing out metaphysics with my Britlit teacher. The Lord's strange rescue arrived in the form of a floppy golden retriever named Lucy, the campus mascot. My teacher was sitting next to me on the couch, and I was uncomfortably aware that he was moving closer as he pointed to the Marvell poem in my textbook. His words were sensual and salacious, and I again felt silenced.

Suddenly the door of the lounge opened and Lucy wandered in. Usually friendly and affectionate, she sniffed suspiciously at my teacher and fixed a threatening gaze on him. Just behind Lucy came her owner, a school administrator, who was startled to find us there. It took only one of the burly administrator's glares to bring my English teacher to his feet, sputtering the answer to the unspoken question, "We were just finishing up a little extra help."

I was left with two distinct conclusions about myself. First, I was different from other girls, an alien who ended up in the faculty lounge on a Friday afternoon. And, second, the only name that could explain how I led myself and others into such situations was Dangerous.

Is it really a surprise that I would become an English teacher? At the time I decided to pursue this career, I recognized it both as a desire to please my father and as a movement toward what I was really passionate about: reading and writing and talking with students about both. I did not once connect my job with a calling to loosen tongues. It was in pursuing my own story in answer to the angel's first question to Hagar—"Where have you come from?"—that I began to see the greater story the Author of life had written in me. The past had brought me to a new chapter where I was again being offered the opportunity to say yes or no to the tragedy in my story.

WHERE ARE YOU NOW?

When the Angel of the Lord discovered Hagar behind the bush, he did not ask the obvious question, "Where are you now?" but his questions enabled her to see her sordid state. One of the fruits of story feasting is that the unnamed present begins to take on words as we remember past stories. As I lived out the story of the death of a dream, for instance, two fellow feasters brought my past to bear on my present.

During the week of the class at Mars Hill that so severely disrupted my schema, I had plans to pick up my friend Lalla, one of the women from Moms' Group who had come to Seattle to do the recovery week with Dan Allender. The plan was that I would provide support for her after a tough week. Then, after I finished my class, we would fly back to Florida together.

Our time together turned out differently. At the appointed hour, I drove to the ferry station. Lalla got in the car, and I burst into tears. My friend had lived a tragic story of betrayal and loss that had muted her lovely voice. As she had shared her story with me, I offered her an insight into her name. In Greek, the word *lala* means "to say or to speak." Over the years I had watched as Lalla recovered her lost language and began to speak of her suffering. That weekend, she offered herself to me as a living story. She didn't say much, but her broken and redeemed story became the sustaining food of remembrance. In her presence I could not deny that God had written me into Lalla's life to help her find her voice and use it.

That same week another woman, aptly named Hope, was feeding me e-mail reminders of how my past had come to bear on the present. She did this without knowing of my struggle. She was merely reflecting on her experiences at Moms' Group:

> I was thinking today about our wild God and the calling he has
> given you. Look how far he has brought you in your journey, from
> a simple vision on a treadmill to this.... Did you ever imagine you
> would be where you are today? He has used you so greatly to encour-
> age, mentor, and inspire weary women looking for some hope.

Hope had read me, and she wrote me. She caught me in my own story. When we gather in community and tell our stories, we can't cheat later and pretend God hasn't written any stories of redemption in our life. Someone will be sure to remember. I wanted to plunge into despair during my course at Mars Hill, but God put before me a living story of redemption in Lalla. As I desired to lose hope, Hope refused me that option. Both women brought reminders in the present that would prevent me from fleeing from the future.

WHERE ARE YOU GOING?

As we gather in community to celebrate stories, we read the past, we name the present, and we dream the future. Feasting on stories together, we offer one another the love that gives us courage to write again.

The day after the story feast where I read my story of loss and the perceived death of a dream, an e-mail arrived. A dear and brilliant woman, a PhD candidate in science education, sent this word:

Hi Elizabeth,

I was excited about seeing you last night, full of curiosity about your time in Seattle and hoping that things had gone well for you. Needless to say, that wasn't the case. It was painful, watching you cry.

I wanted to say, "Don't give up on your dream," but I don't know God's will for your life. But certainly, don't let one small group of people destroy your vision. There may be a purpose behind the pain and challenges that you faced.

I wish I had more knowledge of the Bible so I could quote Scripture, but I can say that those people were wrong. Listen to the message, whatever it may be, and trust in the Lord. I'm still looking for answers myself, sometimes wondering if I should just quit everything and take up other passions. But I keep plodding along until God tells me otherwise.

Praying for peace,
Elaine

I knew the tremendous risk Elaine took to write those words. She had come to Moms' Group broken and frightened, much like the stray dog she compared herself to in a beautifully written tale she had offered to us at an earlier feast:

The little dog who entered my life so desperate for love taught me many things about love and my relationship with my own heavenly Father. In many ways, I was like Peanut, a victim of my own past, hurting, and in need of love. I would snap at people and didn't trust people. But I wanted love and acceptance, and I wanted to give love. Just as I was determined not to give up on Peanut, so too was God determined not to give up on me. With soft hands and loving heart, [God] gently wooed me, even when I bit his hands. Just as I attempted to heal Peanut physically and emotionally and give her a life of luxury, in the way of air-conditioning, a doggie bed, and regular meals, so too did God attempt to touch my life with his love.[7]

In her story of Peanut, Elaine offered me a freeing way of looking at my struggle. I differed with the teacher at Mars Hill. I felt there were many problematic issues in the way he dealt with women in our class. But once again, I had allowed myself to be silenced. In doing so, I had turned hard and mean. I nipped at him and at some of my classmates. It's very likely that I myself created a portion of my bad experience and the perception that my dream was dying.

Elaine's letter was humbling, but it gave me hope. The gift of love propels us to return to our story, pick up our pen, and write again.

When I shared my story in community, I came to see that my "Death of a Dream" story was in fact a "Story of Flight." Within the negative experience at Mars Hill, I felt the dangerous encroachment of an old story: A tragic story of divorce that dates to my childhood. A failed story of not winning my father back with my words. An abusive story of being used for wicked fantasies by high-school teachers. And finally a story of being shamed and silenced in front of my friends. I despised and longed to forget this story. But my fellow story feasters read my story in a way that invited me to revisit my past, reclaim my present, and rewrite my future.

Various teachers had abused authority and power in a way that led me to believe my words were dangerous tools of seduction. I have since learned that words are indeed dangerous. They are weapons that destroy evil and entice people to the Author of all words. Indeed, the Word made flesh, offered up for us, is God's weapon of choice. In feasting on stories, I have seen that the Author has inscribed his glory in me in a uniquely personal way, transforming the theme of lost words into a passion for loosening the tongues of those who are muted by shame.

Because of the women who have feasted with me, my story is one I no longer wish to deny. I finish writing these words on Resurrection Sunday: Christ our Passover is sacrificed for us. Therefore let us keep the feast.

THE END OF THE BEGINNING (DAN ALLENDER)

When I first met Elizabeth, I had no idea where my story would lead her in the reading, telling, and rewriting of her own story. Nor did I have any idea where her story would transport me. I had no idea, only a sense of hope. And hope is what we eat when we celebrate a story feast.

We human beings are meant to be celebrated. We are meant to be the subject of tears, struggle, and heartache, of raucous laughter, wonder, and joy. We are meant to be birthed in the care of others who know and love our story.

To write and to live, we must suffer alone before the blank screen or empty page. We must develop the discipline necessary for praying, fasting, and giving to others—for writing the story that is to be our life creation. And we must read and offer our writing to others as we receive their work in community. We do this for the sake of the great, glorious, and communal story of God.

Telling Your Story

Elizabeth and Moms' Group at her church learned how to come together for the purpose of feasting on their stories. (If you would like to see the work of the Story Feast in action, please visit www .storyfeast.org.) In what contexts do you feast on stories (for instance, at family gatherings or in a small group at church)? In those contexts, what kinds of stories do you tell?

chapter ten

prayer that reveals

Receiving Your Story, in Awe and Gratitude to God

What would I find in my own heart if the noise
of the world were silenced? Who would I be?
Who will I be, when loss or crisis or the depredations
of time take away the trappings of success,
of self-importance, even personality itself?
KATHLEEN NORRIS

"Let's pray."

When you hear those words, do they invite you or irritate you? Praying is the right thing to do before preaching, teaching, or eating, but how about during lovemaking, playing poker, or shopping at Wal-Mart? And if one is to pray without ceasing, what prayer does one utter before entering Wal-Mart?

We are impoverished if we consider prayer to be a religious activity. In truth, prayer is a rich relational engagement that is fraught with paradox, mystery, absurdity, and storybound drama. As an activity, prayer makes no sense. Why pray to a God who already knows everything? If he knows my thoughts before I even think them, then what's the point? If he does the *real* praying for me through the Spirit, who utters unheard and unspeakable words on behalf of my spirit, then what more can I add?[1]

The answer to these questions is straightforward: God wants relationship. And while stated in just three words, this answer creates even more complexity and oddity. How does my talking to, asking, and informing the Divine lead to a more intimate relationship for either one of us? God simply doesn't talk that much, or if he does, then I am mostly deaf. When I pray, God's response is silence at least 95 percent of the time. Perhaps your prayer life elicits far more words from God. Mine doesn't, but the 5 percent of the time when he has spoken is enough to keep me fumbling with words, addressing the Almighty, and listening for his divine speech-acts.

Prayer tills the soil of the soul and unearths the clods of stories that lie beneath the surface. Prayer exposes and opens our heart. It takes us into a dialogue with God that is often disconcerting. Prayer also becomes the context for receiving from God his presence. It is a conversation that brings us face to face with how he authors us and calls us to write our story. Prayer, in straight talk, is surrender to God's authorship.

NAKED PRAYER

Search me, O God, and know my heart;
    test me and know my thoughts.
Point out anything in me that offends you,
    and lead me along the path of everlasting life.[2]

Two men, one a Pharisee and the other a tax collector, went to the temple to pray. It's interesting that the Pharisee stood and prayed about *himself*. "God, I thank you that I am not like other men—robbers, evildoers, adulterers—or even like this tax collector. I fast twice a week and give a tenth of all I get." In contrast, we read that the tax collector, a reviled social outcast, "stood at a distance. He would not even look up to heaven, but beat his breast and said, 'God, have mercy on me, a sinner.' "[3]

We live between these two kinds of prayer, between gratitude that strays to presumption or desperation that strips away self-righteousness. Are we to be grateful? Of course, but seldom do we permit any blessing to remain as an undeserved gift from God. Instead, we assume that we somehow did something to earn it, and we hold on as if we deserve it. It's the inevitable cycle that we see in the history of Israel. God's people presume upon the blessing of God, which leads to the temptation to possess his gift as a deserved necessity.

But there is also desperation, the troubled longing for personal and corporate transformation. When we're in that state, we utter our deepest and finest prayers. The prayer for mercy asks God to lift our face and remove our stain. Desperation introduces us to our shame, and much of our story involves shame.

In times of desperate prayer, God invites us to love the story he has written in our life, even the chapters that produce shame. No soul can hope to love the story infected with the stain of sin and streaks of sorrow unless the shame withers. And shame will not wither unless we choose to enter *all* of our stories—including the stories that bring heartache. We must enter the narrative naked before God and go there completely open to the story he has written.

Entering the narrative before God means, first, that we must enter prayer as a struggle. We do not merely utter a string of sweet words according to a prescribed sequence, such as adoration, confession, thanksgiving, and supplication. Of course, prayer can be orderly and organized. But the prayer that pleads for exposure and engagement throws our desperation at God's feet and wrestles naked with him for the blessing of a new name. This is prayer that heals.

Healing prayer is a wrestling match, true. But that's not all it is. Beyond a sweaty grappling with God, healing prayer takes our stories of heartache and inserts Jesus into the memory to whiten the stain and take away the anguish. To achieve that end, you must willingly ponder your memories and *fully* study the meaning of those past events. You can't enter only so far and then stop, capping the process by imagining Jesus's loving face bringing comfort and good cheer. That's not wrestling with God, nor is it healing prayer.

Certainly, Jesus does bring healing. And he does smile on us and bring comfort. So there is a place for imagining Jesus's face in scenes of our past suffering. But many choose this path as a type of spiritual lobotomy. Such imaginings can be a shortcut to shelving the story as a finished product, never to be taken down and read again.

Shelving the story replaces a deep sense of anguish and anger with tranquillity and peace. That is not Jesus, nor is the removal of anguish and anger a sign of healing. Remove anguish and you remove mercy. Erase anger and you erase a hunger for justice. Jesus doesn't take away anguish and anger; he transforms heartache to passion and anger to righteous defiance. Instead of shelving these unsavory emotions to get them out of sight, Jesus transforms them.

In the same way, God doesn't take away groaning or indignation. Our yes and our no arise from the passion that groaning and indignation conceive. To lose anguish is to be one step closer to robotic inhumanity, as if such a spiritual lobotomy could make a person happier.

Therefore, healing prayer doesn't push suffering off to the side, where it can be safely ignored. Instead, in healing prayer we enter the scene of our tragedies with profound particularity. Healing prayer allows us to name the scene of shame in detail. It doesn't take the pain away by reconstructing the story with a magical substitute—the image of Jesus sitting at our side as we are being harmed. Instead, healing conversations with God lead straight into the unstated gaps of the story that we find far too painful to name. It goes where none of us would dare go without Jesus, but it doesn't use Jesus to deflect the pain of the story.

As we get close to the particular element in the scene that marked us most deeply with shame or sorrow, the dissociation that has supplied our safe and empty peace will reappear. Right then, when we are tempted to turn our back to the pain and flee, we must wrestle with our refusal to turn to God and rage or repent. What do we want most: God or the hollow peace of our own control?

To cast Jesus into the scene too quickly prevents our heart from entering the real war. It is not that we don't think Jesus was present. We know he was. It is the fact he was present and *did nothing to stop the harm* that steeps our rage in self-righteousness. Why does he not answer these questions:

- Why didn't you keep my parents from divorcing?
- Why didn't you stop the abuse?
- Why didn't you prevent the accident?

God will answer no such questions, no matter how often and how passionately we ask. Instead, he invites us to weep with him and receive his mercy. And he roars in anger with us and calls us to take up his sword to wage war against that which broke our heart.

Healing prayer simultaneously soothes us and arouses us to battle. Jesus appears as both lion and lamb—furious and bold, gentle and meek. Prayer heals when we submit our story to his sorrow, when we join his tears and surrender to his anger and embrace our calling to destroy evil. It is not a mere psychological exchange or erasure of the past; it is instead a transformation of our heart that enables us to enter reality with more honesty and hope.

Without naked prayer, we can never get to the depths of our story and unearth the data of our heartache. So we must pray as we walk and as we write. We must submit ourselves to God when we ask another person to pray for us. And we must come to understand that telling our story to another person is as much prayer as when we close our eyes and fold our hands. Prayer is a posture of dialogue that expects God to speak in the mix of our conversation. Otherwise it is impossible to imagine what it means to pray always.[4]

Our stories take on greater shape and clarity when we pray. Certain elements of the story bring us new sorrow and anger and increase our connection to the past as well as our hunger for the future. Prayer sensitizes, arouses, and moves us. The result is more tears and more desire. As we pray with this kind of honesty, we walk the terrain of heartache and shame with greater freedom. Naked prayer brings us eventually to the point of haggling with God. Naked prayer compels us to demand of God a different story.

HAGGLING IN PRAYER

It is nearly impossible to grasp the nature of haggling in a country that is spotted with strip malls and department stores. But if you shop in the Middle East for meat or a piece of art, you'll haggle. The process involves artful give-and-take in which both parties posture as losers yet feel they are the inevitable winner. It is the craft of win-win that is a dance of conflict, compromise, and honor.

Likewise, prayer is haggling. It is negotiation with God. And God wants us to negotiate with him regarding our future story. But to even consider doing this is absurd. God is God: Almighty, Creator, Sovereign. We are marred humans, flawed, sinful, sometimes too stupid for words. How can we negotiate with the Divine? The negotiations begin when we start taking him at his word.

When you read Scripture, it becomes clear that dialogue changes God; it alters his perspective, it changes his mind. He tells us to awaken him as if he is an unrighteous judge. Then he dares to repent. He repents because of prayer, and so do we.[5]

Of course, you and I repent of our sin, but God repents of something other than sin because he is not capable of sin. He is only capable of becoming sin on our behalf. Does that make sense? Not really. Is it logical and reasonable? Not at all. God's repentance can certainly be explained away by a theology embarrassed by the Word, but it forces us to bump up against the nonlinear pretzel logic of narrative. God changes his mind after we pray? It doesn't make sense, but he does change.

And as we engage the narrative, it somehow does make sense—or at least it makes for a gripping story. Consider God's puzzling conversation with Moses. God wanted this thick-tongued shepherd to march into Pharaoh's palace and tell the pagan king that the God of the Hebrews wanted him to forgo the services of a slew of slaves. God blazed his command to Moses in transcendent neon. And Moses simply said, "I'm not up for the task."

An argument ensued in which the Creator humbled himself. He reminded Moses that he is the Maker of the mouth and the Writer of each person's story, as if Moses had somehow forgotten who God is. Moses didn't flinch, even before the fire of God's glory. He declined to go to Pharaoh. So God came up with an alternative—providing Moses with a mouthpiece.

Their dialogue is beyond odd.

Moses: "O LORD, I have never been eloquent, neither in the past nor since you have spoken to your servant. I am slow of speech and tongue."

God: "Who gave man his mouth? Who makes him deaf or mute? Who gives him sight or makes him blind? Is it not I, the LORD? Now go; I will help you speak and will teach you what to say."

Moses: "O Lord, please send someone else to do it."

By now, God is losing patience, but still he caves in to Moses's arguments.

God: "What about your brother, Aaron the Levite? I know he can speak well…"[6]

We can learn from this strange dialogue: we pray to awaken our sleeping God. We pray to remind him of our suffering and to beseech him to alter the course of our story. We pray to the Almighty to take notice of the unrighteous, to stop them in their tracks, and to break their backs and their will. Prayer is an attempt to get, as Moses did, the best bargain we can from Almighty God.

This sort of talk offends people, whether they're listening with religious or rational ears. God is not a corner shopkeeper, eager to discount his price in order to make a sale. Nor is he fickle. Indeed, the Bible makes it clear that God doesn't change, nor is there any variation or "shadow of turning" in him.[7] Yet God repents. Is this mere anthropomorphic language, or is it beyond our comprehension that the unchanging God who doesn't repent like a man nevertheless repents like God and changes without altering the core character of his being? I vote for the latter.

God told Moses his name: "I AM WHO I AM." Apparently he is who he is. And he is unchangeable in the mystery of his willingness to change his mind, alter his judgment, revoke his anger, and concede to the story we wish to write. The guarantee of his unwavering character is that your story will not go awry. God will use the words and the wrath of humans to praise his name.

So what does this really mean for your story and for mine?

God speaks, and we must trust not only what he says but that he speaks at all. In the same way, he writes our life from the foundation of the earth, but he doesn't let us glimpse his novel until long after we have written our life and met him face to face.

Two core statements the Bible makes about God clarify his authorship. One states unequivocally that he is the Author of every moment of our life. He is my authority because he has written my life for his purposes. I am the clay tablet, the blank slate in his hands.[8]

But while God is our Author, the Bible makes it clear that God is not the author of sin. He did not set into motion Adam and Eve's rebellion, flight, and fight against him. He did not solicit and urge Cain to spill the blood of his brother. He didn't cause Hiroshima, the Holocaust, or your next-door neighbor's boy to break into your garage.

All sin is the province of the dark kingdom. And what prompted the citizens of the dark kingdom to flee from the light to turn into shriveled unpersons of hate, lust, and envy? We don't know and will likely never fully comprehend. Evil malignantly grows from the freedom we possess to love or not love. Love would be meaningless if we didn't also have the option to *not* love.

If love is coerced, it is at best obedience that fears reprisal and at worst insincere manipulation to gain what the object of our love can give us. But genuine love arises in the complex interplay of desire and gratitude. I want and God gives. He gives so far beyond what I need that I am caught in the swirl of mouth-open awe and stunned gratitude. We write best when, in loving God and being loved by him, we are thrown into the space of awe and gratitude.

Praying with Awe

Negotiations with God ought to be conducted with awe. How can a mere man or woman be talking to God, let alone arguing with him? How can I be invited to name that I believe God is asleep, uncaring, or unrighteous? It's more than mortal minds can fathom. I would never speak such words to a powerful national leader who had the power to destroy me, so why would I do so before the throne of omnipotent God?

Awe comes with a sense of the inconceivable reversal of relationship that God invites us to enter. He wants us to write our story in concert with him but also in opposition to him. Our fight against his apparent lethargy takes us into realms of injustice that he seems to have ignored. The deep-hearted no that he has planted in us is to some degree a fight against his seeming inactivity. The story we write takes us to people he seems to have abandoned. Yet God brings himself into the fray through us.

So has God abandoned his people? No, he sent you and me. And it is when we realize he has nudged us into action, to care, to fight, that our awe at his plan takes our breath away. It is all so odd. He builds burdens in us through our own experience of being orphaned, exiled, and widowed. And then he uses those losses to deepen our war with him which, of course, he wins again and again as we surrender to his goodness. In turn, he sends us to live out our burdens with those who need us but who, in the long run, end up bringing us more than we could ever offer them.

In reading more of my own story, I never planned to enter the dark realm of sexual abuse. I vaguely knew that I had experienced some unpleasant sexual moments, but they were long past and without any noticeable effect in my life. And then the fateful moment came when I was asked by a client if I knew much about sexual abuse. With that passing question, the trajectory of my life changed. I didn't know it at that moment, but in my engagement with her story, I found dark moments in my own past beginning to rise far on the horizon. It took years before I could name my own abuse and see the marks of its effect up close, but the God who weaves glory from the single, stained threads of our life was inviting me to pick up my pen and follow him.

Every drop of blood that is shed as we rage against God's inactivity becomes the ink of desire that we use to write a new chapter to his glory. If we don't write in a state of awe, however, then we will settle for writing a tepid story full of comfortable Christian rhetoric. The latter is not a true story. Only awe can compel us to write a story that sings of God's odd and arousing glory.

Praying with Gratitude

The great mystery of coauthoring our story with God is evident in this question: who authors whom? For many years I thought I was helping victims of abuse break free of the bondage of shame. Then it dawned on me that my clients free me far more than I set them loose. The same was true of my children. They were authoring me even as I seemed to be writing their lives. So who is my coauthor? God, most certainly. But others also, because God loves to create in community.

As coauthors with one another, we need to be engaged in an echo of gratitude. I am grateful you are reading this book. You might thank me for being part of writing it. The echo has begun. This book may stir you to begin writing a portion of your life that has been waiting for years to be written. And as your story is read and edited with others, you will serve other souls who will be eternally indebted for your blood and ink. In turn, they will enter the awesome joy of coauthoring their future with God and for his glory.

Perhaps you have labored with a group of friends who love to glory in one another's gifts. You are like a band that plays with passion as a tight ensemble yet easily turns the spotlight to highlight a brilliant solo. And then the individual labor rolls seamlessly back into a unity that serves the whole without forgetting the individuality of the parts.

I served on such a committee at Mars Hill Graduate School that was planning the school's first-ever fall retreat. The people on the committee were diverse in their perspectives and desires. The conversation was rich, heated, and wild.

It came time to plan the retreat's Sunday worship, and it was clear that the event would have so many moving parts that it needed more space than any of the buildings at the site could accommodate. It was decided to create an outdoor cathedral of driftwood in the form of a Celtic cross.

Fall in the Puget Sound area is an iffy weather proposition at best. It could be dry, but it's wiser to bet on Lotto than to wager on dry skies. What if it rained? With that in mind, the question was posed: "What would worship be like if rain was actually invited and viewed not as an interruption or a distraction but as part of the event?" The question stunned me. *Rain is a problem! It interrupts and dampens. It certainly isn't a welcome guest, nor does it enhance. But who says?*

We often make a distinction between worship in a church and worshiping God in nature. What an artificial division, and what a loss! As simple as it may sound to welcome rain into worship, this idea became the freeing gift of inviting the One who brings rain to be part of our worship.

As it turned out, the worship lasted three hours. We told stories. We used art to create remembrances of our time together. We prayed and read and heard the Word of God proclaimed in and through and over the wind and the rain. Yes, it rained. We marked the beginning of our year huddled under blankets, moving to the center of the cross to receive Communion, and singing with the roar of glory that is so near. I left that time humbled by what had been written by the risk of glory.

The greater the gratitude for the presence of God's glory, the greater one will risk when writing a new chapter—whether that chapter has to do with how we will worship or how we will spend the next year of our life. Gratitude snatches us out of the rut of the common and shows us a horizon ahead that demands we create a new path. As we are called forward, however, we must turn back and carefully survey the debris of the past. The past path took us to this summit. Perhaps there were other routes that would have been less costly, but the past has led us to this moment. The new does not take away the anguish of the old. But the new horizon and our passion to pursue it would not have come without our first treading the path of being orphaned, exiled, and widowed.

Perhaps this perspective enabled Paul to write of "light and momentary troubles."[9] The pain of birthing recedes in the glorious glow of what has been born. We will never come to embrace the heartache of our story until we see it profit another human being. Even then the sorrow doesn't leave, but seeing someone benefit from our pain adds hope to that pain, and our gratitude begins to transform our past.

Gratitude also comes as we see that what we've written of our life prompts God to say, "Welcome, my good and faithful servant." As we see our story used for his glory, we are disposed to love what has been written for us to live.

RECEIVING YOUR STORY

Prayer unearths story from the past and brings us naked into a wrestling match with God regarding our future. As God met Jacob to transform him and to mark him with a limp and a new name, so God plans to do so with us through prayer. To pray is to wrestle with God until we surrender to his goodness.

My story will compel me to plead, shout, and cry at God's injustice, lethargy, and disregard. But in the middle of my rage, I can't help but wonder at what kind of God would bear my contempt and not retaliate. How could he endure my haggling, let alone alter his plan to coincide with mine? In the face of such inconceivable grace, I can't help but fall at his feet with incredulity. The Almighty, Sovereign, Creator God is also the most humble Being we will ever know. And engaging in naked prayer with our humble God humbles us. But what humbles us most is the enormity of his love for us.

It is in surrendered silence that God speaks love. It is when I have brought to him the shredded strands of my story—when I am ashamed, angry, defiant, and afraid—that he calls me to hear what can be written but can't be explained. He speaks love.

There have been times when I've opened my eyes abruptly as I prayed without words, open and present before God's grace, because I felt a goodness surrounding me that sent a chill of joy throughout my body. The light in my body was palpable. Psychological state? Synaptic release of serotonin? Presence of God? Why must I choose from among these? Could it not be all three and more? All I know is that my body received the pulse of love that is consonant with sitting in the warm lap of a father, feeling the warm embrace of a brother, and melting into the warm caress of a lover.

Some of our stories describe abandonment, betrayal, and ambivalence. We experience those losses and assaults as orphans, strangers, and widows. Should it surprise us, then, that God wants to make himself known as the Father who protects the orphan, as the Brother who encourages the stranger, and as the Lover who cherishes the widow? The Triune God who is One wants to redeem our story and restore with his love what our story took from us.

The Father brings meaning to our orphaned heart by helping us catch a glimpse of his plan for our life. He has prevented our story from being swallowed by evil, and he has given us the deepest desire of our heart—himself. The orphan now has a Father.

The Son brings courage to our exiled heart by suffering all that we will endure and doing so completely without sin. Jesus has taken the lead in the battle and is not ashamed to call us his brother and sister. He befriends us, those who are aliens and strangers. As he befriends the stranger, he himself is taken outside the gates of the city to be the ultimate Stranger in order to keep us from ever again being alienated from his Father.

The Spirit brings tenderness to our widowed heart by caressing us with his tender touch and arousing us to love and good deeds. The Spirit woos us with the words of a lover, inviting us to a union with God that is intimate, passionate, and fruit bearing. We are not alone, nor will we be left without a voice.

It is through prayer—naked, argumentative, thankful, awestruck prayer —that God intends to weave the magic of love through our broken and bloody story. Then, when we fast, our story starts to gain the momentum to become real.

Telling Your Story

Prayer is a plea for God to take the stories that were meant for evil and use them for good, to write something beautiful out of tragedy. Through the pain, God makes us more compassionate and strong for the sake of those who suffer. "Jesus doesn't take away anguish and anger; he transforms heartache to passion and anger to righteous defiance." But for that transformation to take place, we must first wrestle with God.

What parts of your story are laced with such shame that you will not wrestle with God over them? Where have you seen your heartache used by God for the good of another person?

chapter eleven

the fruit of fasting

The Hunger That Opens Space for Others

When I think of fasting, I would define it as
abstaining from anything that fills the space
inside us that God longs to occupy. Any idols
can be fodder for fasting: TV, e-mail, food. The
heart of a fast is stepping back from life as it
is and conceiving life as it could be.

HEATHER WEBB

I awakened at 3:30 a.m. It was not a worry-rising—there was no crisis. It
was not an abrupt thrust into wakefulness due to an unsettling dream. I
hadn't even had pizza for dinner. I simply woke up, and I felt a prompting

183

to rise. But I tend not to obey those moments. I figure if God wants me to rise, he can yell just a little louder. He usually doesn't.

I've been told that I might be missing moments of significant revelation. Or it may be that at those times I am uniquely called to pray—and that disaster might prevail if I don't. But I figure if I'm that necessary to the kingdom of God, we're all in big trouble. So I usually just go back to sleep.

But not that morning. That time I got out of bed.

I rose easily when the words came to me: "Give up sleep." I went downstairs and turned on a light along with our fake fire. The flames are even and monotonous, but they flicker enough to hypnotize. I let my mind wander, and eventually it found a resting spot—a video of my biological father and me, copied from an old home movie made on Christmas morning when I was three. My father had a little more than six months to live, and it would be many years before I would know that he had even existed.

As I sat staring at the flames, I pictured my father as he is on the video—handsome, dark, surprisingly gentle, and attentive. He is also strangely distant from the camera and, I suspected, from the woman who was making the home movie. In the video I am little, persistent in my play with the folds of his bathrobe. I'm searching for something without giving it my direct attention. All three of us—the filmmaker, the father, and the little boy—are lost in three separate worlds. The tree sparkles, and the presents are strewn around the floor. It is meant to be a happy scene. But as I projected the movie in my mind, I could barely watch without screaming.

I felt a sudden, strong urge: "Take and eat." It was too disconcerting to continue watching the home movie, so I decided to make some coffee, toast with jam, and cereal. But the voice said, "Give up food." This time the voice felt audible, though it was not. The war was on. Would I remain sitting there, feeling the glowering hunger, or would I feed the inner ache with toast and hot coffee, dulling the presence of my biological father who was gone before I ever got to know him?

I chose to fast. And the next three-plus hours were some of the hardest I can remember. It was as if God chose to parade across the flickering fire the faces, images, and scenes of one betrayal after another. I witnessed once again the betrayals related to older men whom I had known through Boy Scouts, football, college, seminary, first ministry. These were mentors and fathers.

I don't know what Peter experienced when God gave him a vision of a cloth coming down from heaven with unclean animals on it and then told him to eat. Was it a hallucination or a dream or an event as tangible and discrete as filling up your gas tank yesterday afternoon? And does it even matter? The cloth descended, and on it were animals that Peter had been taught since he was a boy were unclean. But then a voice told him to eat. What do we do with the voices that tell us to eat or to give it up—especially when the directive goes against every fiber of our being?

As I stared into the fire, the stage descended, and on it were the characters of my play.

I fasted for nearly four hours from sleep and food—from the ever-present blessing of provision—so that I could make a space on the stage for the characters of my stories to speak their parts. They spoke lines I knew, since I had been there when the words were first spoken. But the sequence of the characters' appearances and the force of their words were new and horrible. I was called to enter a desert of death and deceit, a wasteland of broken promises, to make room for God's entrance from stage left.

I sat there and watched a newsreel of my life. Each face and presence spoke an ache that excavated my emptiness. As the hours progressed, I stopped feeling haunted, hungry, or even sad. The pain had flashed like lightning bursts, the wind howled, and the rain pelted me until I was bruised.

I had weathered the storm, and it had passed. Now the voices remained, and those who had betrayed me remained betrayers. But I was at home with them, because alongside me was the greatest of all betrayers—God. The One who had turned his back on his own Son.

Fasting from any nourishment, activity, involvement, or pursuit—for any season—sets the stage for God to appear. It was my season to feel the rush of story and to make a place inside to receive it. But I had no idea why. Fasting is not a tool to pry wisdom out of God's hands or to force needed insight about a decision. Fasting is not a tool for gaining discipline or developing piety (whatever that might be). Instead, fasting is the bulimic act of ridding ourselves of our fullness to attune our senses to the mysteries that swirl in and around us. Sometimes God shows up. And sometimes he feeds us. And every now and then he throws his wild glory before us like bursting constellations, and it's all we can do to wait for him to leave, lest we be destroyed in his presence.

So I sat in this busy, empty room watching God consume some of my deepest hurt with the lightning fury of his fierce presence. There was nothing I could do but surrender to being the theater of his odd and wild ways. Ultimately, however, I would confess that his bread of bitterness is better than the sweetest fare I have ever tasted. I took and ate, and it was good.

My wife came downstairs around 7:00 a.m. and asked what I'd been doing. I told her, "Ridding myself of this earth...just space travel."

She raised an eyebrow.

RELINQUISHMENT

When I miss a meal, I have to remind myself that I likely won't die. It's no surprise, then, that I'm more familiar with the finer points of the molecular structure of helium than I am with fasting. I don't like being hungry. And I don't like absence, letting go, departure, or living in the middle ground between life and death. Fasting enters the terrain of loss for the sake of hope, and I'm not at all comfortable in that territory.

I once heard an expert on fasting say, "You have to develop a heart to fast." I don't doubt that to be true, though my spirit is willing but my body is weak. Fasting requires relinquishing one's body at the point when it most craves satisfaction. Fasting is a testing, a cleansing, and a desert struggle with the idols that dull the body's keen awareness that we are not home. Fasting calls us to enter our orphaned, exiled, and widowed heart. And none of us wants to go there.

Similarly, none of us wants to relinquish our story to God, but we must. I don't know what that means, exactly. But I do know it when I don't relinquish it. When I cling to my pain, it feels like hoarding. I remember a betrayal, and I wallow in the unrighteousness of the hurt. I turn it around and around in my mouth and savor its bitter juices. If someone came to clear my plate from the table, I'd snarl and guard my prey. It's mine! And no one can know the depth of the wound.

To relinquish my hurt involves asking God not so much to take the pain away but to enter the sacred ground. Like a procedure that involves opening a wound further to promote healing, the cure seems as painful as the disease. We want our painful story healed without realizing that a greater pain will come as the Physician begins to cut and clean out the infection.

Fasting is a part of this cutting and cleaning. And fasting begins with the acknowledgment that I've tried to be the Father to my own orphaned loneliness; the Son to my own estranged confusion; and the Holy Spirit to my widowed shame. I've fed myself bread—much of it legitimate and good—yet it could not salve the wound or fill the emptiness.

I may know this to be true to the depths of my synaptic core, but my stomach doesn't. My stomach is a god. My dumb stomach knows only two states: full and empty. And it must be led to experience what my soul already knows—we are not at home. I know my body won't go there without being prompted.

My body must come to know God's fatherly provision, and that understanding comes in the quiet that follows the onslaught of the storm. The Father brings shalom that passes all understanding—meaning that the peace he gives is not something we know rationally. Instead, knowing his peace comes through experience that is not mere cognition. As we submit our body to God's fatherly presence, we open space within us for his kind of peace. It is a peace that enters paradox as the field of play. And such is the paradox behind Scripture that says, without irony: "You meant evil against me, but God meant it for good."[1]

I know that peace when my Father soothes me in his lap and bridges all my sorrow to his glory. I must relinquish my fight enough to see through the mist of mystery. His presence is barely discernible, but I find its outline in the contours of my story. So will I surrender to my Father's comforting of me, an orphan?

I also must come to know God's presence as a friend who walks with me—my Companion and Brother, God the Son. Our alienation aligns us with this ultimate Alien—the Maker of heaven and earth who also was the Despised One of this earth. He is the face at whom we rage contempt. His beard has been plucked, and he knows shame—but he is not bound by it.[2] He mocks shame; he refuses to remain quiet in his aloneness. In fact, he revels. He seizes the advantages of being a fool and beckons us to shed our rags and run and play without fear. My body is meant to romp and race with him. I am a stranger and an alien who now has a Brother.

Yet my body needs more than parental *agape* love and the *philia* of a shame-free friend and companion. I am also made for the sensual, erotic embrace of a Lover. God the Spirit winsomely woos, allures, and ravishes us. The Spirit is our Lover. The Spirit is wisdom who is personified in the book of Proverbs as a woman of enormous beauty and wiles. She invites us into her house with fragrance and the promise of warmth, touch, satisfaction.[3]

Fasting prepares my heart to receive a Father, a Friend, and a Lover. It helps me name the condition of my soul, which has been filled with counterfeits and which now aches for the real One. In many ways, fasting is a form of detoxification. It begins to break our addictive attachment to lesser gods to make room for the one God. Fasting has for millennia been associated with sin, repentance, and cleansing. So it's no wonder that when we fast, we initially feel furious and out of control. Fasting reveals how wed we are to the power of things—even legitimate, good things.

As hunger swirls and the early storm of fasting begins to brew, we have an opportunity to sit in and with our body. And if we listen, we will hear the countless voices of suffering we have silenced in our busy flight from our wounds. We can let them speak and let them name their heartache. Fasting releases toxins of loneliness and shame. But don't turn from the stories or the characters that begin speaking, even shouting. Listen, receive, and submit. In due season, the pain will quiet and your heart will be invited to embrace all the stories of your life. Relinquishment leads to an intensification of sense and sensibility.

INTENSIFICATION

As we fast and even slightly break the hold of our stomach-filling idolatry, our senses become more acute. And the more sensually aware we are of the world around us and in us, the more sensible we become. Fasting intensifies the colors, sounds, smells, tastes, and touch of life.

Paul brilliantly assessed the effect of addictions. He wrote,

> So I tell you this, and insist on it in the Lord, that you must no longer live as the Gentiles do, in the futility of their thinking. They are darkened in their understanding and separated from the life of God because of the ignorance that is in them due to the hardening of their hearts. Having lost all sensitivity, they have given themselves over to sensuality so as to indulge in every kind of impurity, with a continual lust for more.[4]

Addictions make us dull. We are meant to be sensitive, but as we deaden our senses, we compensate by trying to bring them back to life through more indulgence. The more we do so, the more we need to do so. We are on a cheap pony ride that turns in tighter and tighter circles until the tether rope is wound so tightly around the center pole that neither pony nor rider can take even one more step. Thus, we are immobilized.

An addiction is a tragic two-edged sword. Every addiction dulls the soul while simultaneously increasing an insatiable craving for more. The result is an indulgence in a perverse sensuality that seems as if it will create life, but over time it actually kills desire. The result is bondage, an attachment that suffocates rather than frees one to breathe.

Sadly, most people assume addictions are the domain of the undisciplined or the socioeconomically deprived. Such an assumption, of course, never looks below the surface at our craven idolatries of consumerism, greed, codependency, schedule obsession, and mania with power and reputation. Addiction touches us all.

Fasting brings us to a suffering surrender, and if we continue fasting, it will inevitably lead to quiet. The quiet is not quiescence. The quiet is more like the pregnant millisecond before the starter's pistol fires. The body is tensed but not tight; it is prepared, leaning into the sound that is about to pierce the air and call forth a burst of passion and movement. Fasting is far more than letting go; fasting anticipates the air being split by the coming presence of the thunderclap God. Some day he will awaken. He will not neglect to hear the cries of his creation forever. Fasting intensifies our desire for God and the capacity to hold desire for others.

Desiring

At first fasting intensifies hunger; then it quiets both the heart and body; and then increases a desire that can rightly be called "homesickness." We are told that Jesus will not drink of the vine nor eat of the earth until we have joined him at his table. He fasts and longs. How does he endure another day without eating or drinking? His words define the nature of a true fast: "I have eagerly desired…"[5]

We are to feel the pulse of our desire. Consider this example: The desire to escape the humdrum of work often hides a deep dissatisfaction with our career. What happens if we admit we hate our work? That acknowledgment may compel us to ask how we fell into the rut. These questions and answers, in turn, may expose the truth that we work merely to put bread on the table for our family. Next, that boredom may compel us to face why we married our spouse. Sadly, too often we married our spouse far more for security and expectation of fulfillment than because of passion or calling. Now, if we look too closely, we risk the relationship. And we risk financial struggle if we confess that our work is for nothing more than a paycheck.

I do not advocate running away from one's work or one's spouse, though desire aroused ruins conventional complacency. And what will be left if complacency is eschewed? What happens if we take a close look and find that the life of the elder brother is pointless?[6] We either give ourselves over to empty pleasures, or we find a deeper pulse of passion and purpose that has marked us from our story.

Will we embrace the desires God has ignited? Desire, once aroused, calls us to dream again, and all dreams require fasting. For me, fasting often comes with simple choices. I can write this chapter while I'm on this plane, or I can choose to watch the in-flight movie. For the weekend athlete, the choice to develop a great fadeaway jumper requires the dreamer to fast from other more pleasurable activities, like leaving the gym to carouse with friends or sitting on the couch and eating unhealthy snacks while watching basketball on television.

We must nourish the truest desires of our heart and then risk the bold act required to give our dreams the ground to grow.

Holding Desire

When we embrace desire as holy and honorable, we then offer the same respect to others and their desire. The more we love our desire to serve and sashay with our God, the greater our commitment to help others embrace their desire. It's the way we're made. We love to give away what we are given. We love to offer what we have received—whether it's a CD of a new band, tips about a great new restaurant, or a book that changed our life. We are natural evangelists.

We can therefore become the sacred space where other people can name their desire. We can offer ourselves to help others explore desire, and that exploration can be done only in the language of story. A friend may want to buy a condo at the beach to get away from the exhaustion of his work. If you know the ache related to your job and have entered the sto-ries, dreams, heartache, and characters that came with that struggle, then it's likely there will be more room within you to hold his struggle. When you have fasted long enough to listen to your own story—including its darkest parts—you are better prepared to hear and to hold the stories of others.

So rather than critique a friend's desire or merely affirm it, give it ground to be explored. Ask questions. Listen to past stories and look for links. Offer an interpretation, but only if it is welcomed. If you do offer an inter-pretation, keep in mind the most central question of the Bible: "Where are you, Adam? Will you come forth and name what is true?" If we will answer that question, we will go to God naked and broken to receive his grace. After fasting, after taking away the demands (addictions) and the flight (shame), then in the quiet we can answer the core questions of desire: *Where am I? Who am I? And what do I want to become?*

Those core questions are key to decision making. Of course, there is nothing inherently immoral about owning a beach condo. But first, desire and story need to be explored. Before a friend purchases a place where he can get away from a home that is not a place of rest, he must ask why his life in general and his home in particular prevent rest. His answers may be standard: "My life is stressful because I'm working really hard while the market holds out." Or her "reasons" may be connected to her story: "My family couldn't survive if I didn't contribute to our income." Will you hold a friend's desire with all its deceit, fear, and ugliness? Will you hold it and lift it to the face of God? Fasting prepares your heart to hold the desires of others and lift them to the face of God in prayer.

Fasting removes the boulders and tills the ground of our heart for sow-ing. The fruit of true fasting is always an engagement with our truest no and yes. And we find and expend our deepest passions in the face of injustice and darkness.

Centering

Fasting deepens our surrender and increases our passion for God—but so what? For some people fasting is nothing more than a spiritual exercise that at best connects them more firmly to God. It may make the person more alive and committed to God, but beyond the subjective value and perhaps some fallout of good for those nearest to the penitent—so what?

True fasting centers us in the heart of God for the sake of those who are orphans, strangers, and widows. From beginning to end the Bible is about justice. To fail to see the social engagement of the gospel is to be blinded to the deepest and truest meaning of Christ's death and resurrection. The gospel is the shalom of God offered to every tongue, tribe, and nation, an invitation to be received into a new kingdom and to follow the King of kings in establishing a holy priesthood that worships God in spirit and truth. Furthermore, salvation is an invitation to every part of our being, including our body, relationships, money, children, reputation, space, and time.

So if you know God, then you are involved in setting free those who are hamstrung by injustice in any of its forms. The prophet Isaiah stripped the religious elite of his day down to their naked hypocrisy when he exposed their pretentious piety and fastidious fasts. And he named what God desires for a fast:

No, the kind of fasting I want calls you to free those who are
wrongly imprisoned and to stop oppressing those who work for

you. Treat them fairly and give them what they earn. I want you to share your food with the hungry and to welcome poor wanderers into your homes. Give clothes to those who need them, and do not hide from relatives who need your help.

If you do these things, your salvation will come like the dawn. Yes, your healing will come quickly. Your godliness will lead you forward, and the glory of the LORD will protect you from behind. Then when you call, the LORD will answer. "Yes, I am here," he will quickly reply.

Stop oppressing the helpless and stop making false accusations and spreading vicious rumors! Feed the hungry and help those in trouble. Then your light will shine out from the darkness, and the darkness around you will be as bright as day. The LORD will guide you continually, watering your life when you are dry and keeping you healthy, too. You will be like a well-watered garden, like an ever-flowing spring.[7]

Isaiah's words take my breath away. Here is the nature of a true fast. All the bread you save is to be given away to those who are hungry. House the stranger and clothe those who are naked. Release the political prisoners. And when relatives call forth our care because they share our blood, we are not to pull the curtains tight and pretend we aren't home. Instead we are instructed to engage with the faces and the stories of those around us who have been ravaged by lust and silenced by violence. Our fasting is meant to make us heirs with the downtrodden because that is who we are.

The Isaiah passage goes on to affirm what we intuitively know to be true: our hunger aligns us with beggars and thieves, with the undesirable and the broken. And once aligned with them, we are not called only to help the poor dears; we are invited to name our own poverty and need. If we heed that call, then we are invited to join other orphans on our Father's lap as together we call him Abba.

As we give our bread and clothes to the hungry and the naked, we are freed of the curse of addictive possession. But don't think I'm advocating merely giving to the poor. It's easy (yet still infrequent) to give a donation of undesired clothes to the local thrift shop or a token few dollars to the bell-ringing Santa and feel as if we've done our duty. Or we might expand our horizon and serve food at a soup kitchen or be part of building a home for a needy family. All such gifts are not only acceptable, but choice offerings to God.

Still, Isaiah is clear on the extent and full meaning of seeking justice for the orphan, widow, and stranger, because every one of us is an orphan, a widow, and a stranger. The passage is simple and elegant: will you make space in yourself for those who need you, and then will you give from your excess? Once you welcome and share with someone who is avowedly hungry, naked, burdened, and wandering, your life will never be the same. The person may be a prostitute sold into the sex-slave trade or a multimillionaire entrepreneur. The hungry come in all forms.

Welcome them. Stretch out your arms and share. Sit at a table and eat and talk together. Once the conversation begins, if your heart has fasted and there is space in you to welcome and share stories, you will experience the most exquisite benefit: as God promised, you will become a watered garden.

In the ancient Near East, water was at a premium. Growing a garden—just trying to keep a few plants alive—would often require the huge investment of labor necessary for hauling water from a well. So the image of a well-watered garden was a metaphor for Eden. The paradox ought not to be lost on us modern Westerners. Fasting takes us to the desert, to the arid emptiness that is the space where we enter into a mortal fight with God in order to participate in a glorious surrender to him. When we enter the desert, though, God honors us by turning the dusty terrain east of Eden into a shalom, a denouement, a taste of Eden.

A WATERED-GARDEN STORY

This story of my fast may seem slight and silly to you, but I offer it nonetheless.

I was teaching a sexual-abuse seminar when I was exhausted from the rigors of a just-ended academic year. As I taught, I felt that I was stumbling. The night before the seminar began, I got to the hotel late, ate an unnecessary dessert, fell into bed, and watched television for several hours, flitting between channels as though I were looking for the Holy Grail.

The next day on the phone with my wife, she said to me, "Why don't you give up television for the rest of the time and fast for dinner and the rest of the evening?" I was furious. She clearly had no idea of the degree of exhaustion or demand that had taken hold of me. I certainly did not need this additional opportunity to suffer. (Nothing, of course, could have been further from the truth.)

Reluctantly, however, I did what my wife suggested. The first evening was anything but glorious. I ached and raged. My prayer was self-absorbed and my mind wandered. When I finally went to bed, my stomach ached, and every time I started to fall asleep, it nudged me with the reminder that I was hungry. I felt like a fool—swinging between abject contempt for being so godless and foolishness for this act of contrition and hope that only seemed to increase my sin and despair. At 2:00 or 3:00 a.m., I finally fell into periodic slumber.

The next morning I taught from 9:00 until 10:30 a.m. When the seminar group took a break, the host had an announcement to make, so I made my way to the men's room and sat in a stall just to get away from people. My efforts all seemed ridiculous. Finally I mustered enough courage and strength to reenter the realm of conversation about abuse and God's healing plan.

Seconds after I stepped outside the restroom door, a middle-aged Korean woman asked me for a few minutes' time. She stood at about four foot ten, and she was severely handicapped. She asked a brief question, and I answered it. Then she looked at me and softly said, "God has taken me from a dark world into a light and hope that I never thought possible, and he used your life to do so."

There is a joy in knowing our life has been used for good. But in this moment, the quiet of her words amidst the noise of my own heart caused me simply to stare. Then she told me her story:

> I grew up in an orphanage in Korea until I was ten. It was a dark, lonely, and cruel place. I was abused many times each day. When I was ten, I was taken by American missionaries into their home, and the next six weeks were the happiest of my life. After six weeks my new father began to sexually abuse me, and that lasted until I was eighteen. He intended to keep me as a sexual partner forever, but I fled at eighteen without a penny, and I eventually put myself through college. Now I am a nurse.
>
> I lived from that point until I was forty-two never believing

there would be a day I'd be free of the darkness, shame, and emptiness. And then I read your book *The Wounded Heart,* and I entered
into a fight that seemed harder than the abuse in the orphanage or
even the decade of abuse by my father. It was a war of hope. I hated
you. Several times I destroyed the book and had to buy a new copy.
But over time the Spirit gently and kindly wooed me to see that
God loved me and had written my story for his glory.

Her words were compassionate, but I felt caught in a moment of haunting glory. The woman took my hands in her petite grip and looked into
my face. Once she had my full presence, she spoke: "You are a tired man.
I suspect you want often to quit, but I want to tell you that I am alive and
I know joy. And it is in large measure due to you. Thank you for having
made space in you for me."

I thought I was going to melt. I looked at her eyes, and she was reso-
lute and bold. There were no tears, just a passion and strength that made
me feel as if I were staring into the face of a lion. I felt like a little boy even
though I towered over this small woman, and all I could do was weep. The
tears rose like a breaking wave, and I could no more resist its force than stop
time. What am I to do with a God who chooses to father me through a
middle-aged Korean woman?

Had I made space in myself for this orphan? Somehow, in spite of
myself, I must have opened some sliver for God to use. Was it the pitiable
fast of the night before? Or was it some other moment years earlier? I didn't
know and I didn't care.

The woman put her hand on my arm and said, "Go teach. And don't
quit." I obeyed her face, her strength, and her words. I went to the podium

and gave away the flowering fruit from a well-watered garden that I don't recall planting or laboring to maintain. I gave away food that was first given to me.

If we open our heart to the fast, we will indeed have more to give away than we can fathom.

Telling Your Story

"Fasting from any nourishment, activity, involvement, or pursuit... sets the stage for God to appear.... Fasting is not a tool to pry wisdom out of God's hands or to force needed insight about a decision.... Instead, fasting is the bulimic act of ridding ourselves of our fullness to attune our senses to the mysteries that swirl in and around us. Sometimes God shows up. And sometimes he feeds us."

Describe what you feel when you fast and what, if anything, comes from the fast.

chapter twelve

giving away your story

Allow Your Story to Reveal God

A gift isn't fully realized until it is given away.... We
therefore submit ourselves to the labor of becoming
like the gift.... To have painted a painting does not
empty the vessel out of which the paintings come.
On the contrary, it is the talent which is not in use
that is lost or atrophies, and to bestow one of our
creations is the surest way to invoke the next.

LEWIS HYDE

I never knew space held stories until I left my first counseling practice to
move west. The office furniture had been carried away by the movers, and

I was going to vacuum the carpet and pick up the debris that a decade had left. I walked into the room and felt a wave of sorrow that I hadn't anticipated. What happened next is hard to describe. I closed the door and sat in the middle of the room, and stories came out of the walls to dance and then be put to rest.

It was the last day before my family and I were to leave, and there were countless errands and tasks to complete, but I couldn't move. I sat in the middle of the room for nearly two hours. I suspect if someone had walked in, that person would have presumed I'd had a psychotic break. I wept and laughed. I sat quietly and was carried along on a journey that felt like the midnight travels of Scrooge. I'd simply been minding my own business, but in a flash I was whisked away to see my life.

Life-changing conversations had occurred in that room. God had at times used me to birth heartache into the beauty of hope. More often than not, the people I was supposed to help brought me stories that transformed *my* heart. I was birthed in that office, and I will never be able to repay those men and women. Stories inevitably haunt and guide us; they indebt us.

Indebted to Stories

Whom do you owe? You owe someone—at the very least your mother and father. But most of us owe someone who has birthed us to become who we are. I owe my life to Ray Dillard. Dr. Ray Dillard was an associate professor of Old Testament at the seminary I attended. He taught me that a person can live a wild and edgy life, speak with passion about the Bible, and be deeply honest about one's failures of love. He taught me earthy holiness.

On a trip to Israel, I was one of twenty of Dr. Dillard's students waiting for a plane in Geneva. I had finagled a row of seats in the airport lounge so I could lie down. My head was up against a table that held ten empty beer bottles, and I was smoking a fine Cuban cigar. Dr. Dillard snapped a picture of me and sat down on the edge of one of the seats. He leaned forward and said, "Whatever you do in this life for God, don't forget that you are undeserving of such luxurious grace." His mischievous smile and twinkling eyes took in the scene and branded my soul with his joy. It should not be a great surprise that for me God's face looks remarkably like Dr. Dillard's.

I could never repay my debt to him, in part because he was a hilarious giver, the kind of giver Paul commended in 2 Corinthians 8. There he talked about the Macedonian church that gave with joy. The Greek word for *joy* is the root of our word *hilarity*. Paul's message was, "Give not because you must but because you can." Give, not counting the money going out, but give with abandon and laughter. You need one hundred dollars? Well, here's five hundred. Dr. Dillard lived in the odd ebb and flow of heartache and hope, and he gave the gift of infectious hilarity to many. What made him even more extraordinary is that he didn't indebt me to himself. But he did indebt me to teach the Bible with depth, passion, and joy. He called for my debt to him to be paid to others. Paul did the same many years ago.

In the book of Philemon, one of the most fascinating but seldom-read letters of the New Testament, Paul wrote to a slave owner. Philemon's slave Onesimus had come to know Jesus through Paul's ministry, and Onesimus had served Paul in a Roman jail. Paul wrote a letter and gave it to Onesimus to take to his owner. The letter was intended to mend the breach between slave owner and runaway slave. What makes this story fascinating is that Paul had also been the one used of God to bring the slave owner Philemon into a relationship with Jesus Christ. Philemon and Onesimus were now family. Here's how Paul put it:

So if you consider me your partner, give him the same welcome you would give me if I were coming. If he has harmed you in any way or stolen anything from you, charge me for it. I, Paul, write this in my own handwriting: "I will repay it." And I won't mention that you owe me your very soul![1]

The plot thickened. In a book that is shorter than most chapters found in his other epistles, Paul demolished the foundation of slavery and any other totalitarian regime. He ripped the heart of slavery out of its body without addressing a single word against the evil institution. Instead, he presumed that a new bond of "story" will not only alter a single relationship but also will, in time, destroy the narrative of slavery.

Paul banked on past story—specifically, the story of how God had used him in Philemon's life. That story was the backdrop of a new story: the saving of Onesimus. One story of redemption links to the next. And over time all stories of redemption come to have a common center. The story line may differ, but the result is the same: transformation.

And stories that transform make us bold. Paul is an example. If Onesimus owed Philemon a debt, Paul pointed out that he himself would gladly repay it. He wrote this in his own wobbly, almost unreadable hand, and then he reminded Philemon: "And I won't mention that you owe me your very soul!" It's hilarious. What he said he wouldn't mention, he named with brazen boldness! It is one of the most unbelievably manipulative statements I've ever read. What makes Paul's wiles so endearing, though, is that the benefit is not for his own gain.

Consider the enormity of Paul's message: "I'm sending this runaway slave back to you. He has most certainly cost you something in his absence. And you might think that Onesimus should forfeit his life so that you might have an example for other slaves who might consider running away." But then Paul said, "If you need to kill him or beat him, take my life or rip into my flesh instead. And by the way, speaking of lives, I want to remind you that you owe me your very soul. But whatever you do, do so with freedom and joy." This is hilarious giving.

What if we were to embrace with wonder every person who has spoken our name and written our story—either to glory and God or to horror and hell? In truth we are as indebted to those who hated us and did us harm as we are to those who have gifted us with a faint reminder of God. I am a debtor to those who sexually abused me because they aroused in me fury and defiance against injustice. For that I am eternally grateful. I don't bless their harm, but I do thank God for how he has chosen to use that harm to mold me to live my story.

Every story that we receive as a gift indebts us to enter the teller's story for good. If I listen to your endless tales of vacationing in Cancun, then I expect you to listen to my road woes. And how much more indebted am I when your engagement with my story transforms my life?

So we are to hold each other's stories. When we remember a friend's birthday, we are putting our arms around an event and calling that person's life good. If we go beyond holding to *entering* the story in order to explore and suffer its fullness, then we have the privilege of helping to write and edit the other person's story for the sake of its potential to reveal God.

We must therefore give one another storytelling opportunities in order to create the debt of care. Jesus himself tells a story to compel us to invest in stories.[2] He taught that we are to use all that we have to make friends. Buy a sailboat if you want, but make sure you use it to gain access to other lives and new stories. Want to hang out in a particular coffee shop? Great, just do so for something more than mere caffeine. As we live our story, we are to give away our talents, time, and wealth to indebt others not to ourselves but to the God who writes great stories. We are to use our money wisely and winsomely to invest in gaining access to stories that can transform others and ourselves.

Obviously this activity is different than paying a person (in some form) to be our friend. By definition, that is entering into a form of prostitution. Neither is this activity buying access to people in order to get one's daughter into Harvard. To tell stories to impress or intimidate is to entrap—the opposite of telling stories to set others free. A gift-giving, liberating story tells of innocence lost, tragedy encountered, imagination employed, and the brief and glorious moments of an ending that reminds us again that our story is not finally written by us, but we coauthor it with God. The gift of this kind of story is the deep and fundamental reminder that we are not our own; we are God's. We invest in another when we see ourselves as uniquely privileged and available to join his or her story.

Gabriel Marcel speaks of "availability" as a "being who is ready for anything, the opposite of him who is occupied or cluttered up with himself."[3] Not to be cluttered with oneself means that we have first embraced our life as God's story, whether we understand or even like what he has written.

Further, not to be cluttered with oneself is to embrace enough of our story to say to God and to others, "He is good. And he has written me well." And perhaps even more, being uncluttered calls me to wrestle with those stories that confuse me, the stories I continue to hold at arm's length. We will never be fully at ease with our story, but we can come to love our story profoundly and with more joy. Finally, to be uncluttered is to offer all of who we are, even the parts that are still unredeemed, for the redemption of others. And as we give our story for another's redemption, more often than not the story will eventually return to us a new gift. What we give away often returns with greater goodness than what we originally gave.

The true debt is, of course, never paid solely to the one who first received and embraced our story. We will hopefully return to that person the same care and more, but still our debt is too small if it is only returned to the one who first received us. Instead, the debt is "paid forward." As I hold and dance with your story, my life will be transformed, and I will have a new story to offer others. Sharing stories is a feast of plenty that increases with each sitting. There is always more story to tell, hear, write, and enjoy.

The better our story is read and enjoyed, the more we're called forth to live our story for God's glory, the more we will offer the same to others. We can repay our debt to God only by loving the story he has written in each of our lives. Such a debt summons us to invest in story—in our own story and in the stories of others.

SUMMONING STORIES

> Next came the servant who had received the two bags of gold, with the report, "Sir, you gave me two bags of gold to invest, and I have doubled the amount." The master said, "Well done, my good and faithful servant. You have been faithful in handling this small amount, so now I will give you many more responsibilities. Let's celebrate together!"
>
> Then the servant with the one bag of gold came and said, "Sir, I know you are a hard man, harvesting crops you didn't plant and gathering crops you didn't cultivate. I was afraid I would lose your money, so I hid it in the earth and here it is."

But the master replied, "You wicked and lazy servant! You think I'm a hard man, do you, harvesting crops I didn't plant and gathering crops I didn't cultivate? Well, you should at least have put my money into the bank so I could have some interest. Take the money from this servant and give it to the one with the ten bags of gold."[4]

The owner of the vineyard decided to take a long and most likely very luxurious trip, and before leaving he put some of his investments into the hands of his trusted servants. He chose to divide the investments into unequal amounts with no explanation. Then he departed with no announcement about when he would return.

Do you see God here? God is often absent; he promises to return at his leisure; he divides gifts, talents, and stories unequally; and he expects everyone to risk and multiply what he gave. He will one day hold us accountable for how we invest ourselves in story, in his story.

The parable is sobering. It boils down to "use it or lose it." Grow or you will die. There is no neutrality with God or with life. If your goal is to conserve your wealth and remain safe, then inflation (the economic equivalent to entropy) will eat away at your principle. Risk is inevitable; safety is impossible. The safer you wish to be, the more likely it is that you will die like a deer in the blinding headlights of the approaching God.

We don't really believe this to be true because we see so many people who seem to be living safe and predictable, if somewhat dull, lives. Why can't we keep the safety and live just a little closer to the edge while also whittling away significant clumps of monotony? Isn't that a fair compromise? But we can't make that Faustian bargain, because God has rigged the world. If we're willing to give up all forms of danger and all chances for thrill, then we can keep a worthless safety. The moment, however, that we edge toward passion (in any hobby, task, or relationship), then we've set in motion an irreversible momentum toward God. Passion is always a slippery slope to God that only burrowing into boredom can stop.

In Jesus's parable, one servant chose preservation over risk. He knew the vineyard owner to be highly eccentric, unpredictable, and difficult. (Again, what a picture of God!) So that servant played it safe by burying his story. He hid it because he knew that if he didn't make good use of it, there would be a price to pay. He couldn't have been more correct while being more desperately wrong.

The vineyard owner didn't require success; he called for wisdom, risk, and tenacity. If this servant had invested and lost, there would be consequences, but not without engagement and deliberation. How do I know? Because the answer is in the story. The owner wasn't looking for a financial windfall. He would have settled for 1.5 percent interest earned on the simplest passbook savings account. He just wanted the servant to risk the bag of gold he'd been given.

We're all given gold in the form of our body, face, name, and story. Some of us are gorgeous and brilliant while others are ordinary. Truly, what does it matter? We are simply called to use our "gifts" to plant the fields and gather the crops that are under our stewardship. What does this mean with regard to the gift of our story? To humbly embrace our story, face, and name means to confess the following:

- We are God's story, which means we are expertly written.
- We are called to write our story with God in order to bring him more glory.
- We write our story best by giving our heart away to others whom we honor as more important than ourselves.[5]

- What we give to others is a unique story, a theme that reveals God like no other story can.
- We discover our unique calling and story as we allow others to read us, which happens as we give ourselves away for their good.
- We reveal God best in relationships when we join with God to write and edit one another's story for God's glory.
- Each of our stories is part of the gospel, the Greatest Story. The gospel is our story and the beginning and end of all that we write.

We are summoned by God to seed this earth with our stories, and we are to harvest the fruit that comes from our labor. Our bags of gold give us power and place. No matter our proportion of gold or which realm of conversation it puts us in, we are to be involved in the same story—grow beauty, pluck weeds, and bring the bounty to God as we celebrate his glory with him.

We must know how much money is in our bag so we can name our giftedness. Most of us balk at such a requirement, either fearing a big head or, more honestly, the weight of glory. To confess that we are possessed of certain gifts requires us to use them. And inevitably when we use our gifts, we provoke envy or encounter greater hardship. Again, it is the way God has rigged the world.

Since our stories reveal God, no story is ours alone. All our stories are owned by God and reveal truth; therefore no one has the right to say of his story, "This is too weird, painful, boring, shameful, confusing, or dark; therefore I will bury it." All our stories are meant to be available for the purpose of revealing God and connecting us to one another.

But our story does not need to be told to *everyone*, even the most intimate friends. We are to be guardians of our story, and it is to be given as a gift—not wantonly but carefully. It is a gift to be given only to the right person at the right time for the right reason. Let me offer an example.

My wife and I were talking about how we would use an unexpected income-tax refund. She wanted to have some cosmetic dental work done. I balked. It seemed like a lot of money to spend on something no one could really see. And then she told me a story. I won't tell it to you since it's personal. The story had to do with moments of significant shame when my wife was student teaching. She told me the story, and I wept. My lovely and kind wife was humiliated by a group of girls, and I wanted them to pay for their cruelty. Yet prior to hearing the story I wasn't willing to pay a few hundred dollars to alter something that had caused my wife shame.

Clearly, stories have the power to transform our heart. I agreed to the dental work, and I then asked, "Why haven't you told me this story before?" She said, "It took me twenty-two years to trust you with that story." I felt both sorrow and honor. Why had it taken me so many years to gain her trust? And what had transpired over that season in our life to assure her that I would hold her story with care?

We will never know all the stories of those closest to us. You can work with colleagues for twenty years and seldom know even the most rudimentary stories of how they came to be who they are today. Nevertheless, every story given to us and every story told to another is a precious gift that has the potential to seed us with God.

A STORY GIFT

The story I'm about to tell is actually four stories moving in separate yet overlapping symmetry. It is complex, like all stories, and yet it straightforwardly communicates the truth that the gift of story inevitably takes us to the story of God's gift.

I sat with a dear friend talking about her daughter. The two of us commiserate often about the joys and sorrows of raising and being raised by teenage daughters. In this particular conversation, my friend told me about an art project that marked her daughter. She took a series of photographs of her body and superimposed them over a picture of a cross that she had carved into her arm. The knife wound was superficial but real. It was a mark of violence, and it reflected her deep war with both her body and her faith.

As a parent and a friend, I was horrified. Teenage cutting is on the rise, and I felt nausea and fear as I reflected on how I'd feel if she were my daughter. The art she created was over the edge. Most would consider the act "sick," but I know the young woman, and I know her war will not be in vain. Her story may appear to be dark, but I know her heart bears a light and life that many more conventional lives have long ago lost. I can't wait to see where the marks of passion take her story.

But her mother, my friend, was undone by this. The work of art was beautiful. It is part of her daughter's deep wrestling with a God who has arisen in the darkness of life to fight for her name and calling. The girl's mother loved the art; she hated the agony. What risk is worth taking to create a new way of seeing life? Art, like life, ought not be dangerous or cost us our blood, we presume. But is that true?

As I tried to comprehend the meaning of her daughter's blood, I told my friend that it reminded me of my favorite novel, Chaim Potok's *My Name Is Asher Lev*. She gasped. That is her daughter's favorite novel. The novel tells of a Jewish artist, an exile to his religiously conservative friends and family because he chose to be an artist rather than a rabbi. The novel moves to Asher Lev's even greater crime of using the cross of Jesus in one of his paintings because he feels that it expresses the depths of his family's pain. Asher Lev violates his faith and takes a risk with his art that puts him beyond the pale of his family and faith in order to enter more deeply into his faith. No one else in his community can comprehend, let alone commend, his choice. My friend's daughter, who was away at college, had asked her mom to bring along that novel on the day she showed her mother her art.

One story (that of Asher Lev) broke open a conversation about another story (a daughter's dangerous art). This conversation allowed my friend to wrestle with her daughter's choice and invited her to consider afresh her daughter's dangerous creation. I felt honored to have been part of a moment of revelation. I had offered part of my wealth, and it had already begun to bring dividends.

Before I left, I asked my friend how she felt about a meeting we'd had with another friend. She said, "It was so enjoyable to see you two so playful and apparently having so much fun." I smiled, because I had likewise experienced the time as mischievous and lighthearted. Then she added, "It was as if you were two boys playing together in a stream." My head snapped back as if I had been rear-ended in a highway accident. "What did you say?" She repeated her observation, and I started to turn cold.

The phrase unlocked a story I had never shared with her. The story involves playing with a friend alongside a stream when I was a child. My friend had crossed over the stream while I stayed on the other side. We walked on opposite sides until the water got too deep for me to cross over to his side. Soon two older boys came out of the woods and began to hassle my friend. He called for me to come to his aid, and I froze. The older boys eventually beat my friend to a pulp as I stood apart, too frightened to go to his assistance. It was one of the most cowardly acts of my life, and the image of playing at a stream with another boy threw me into panic. I had to leave the conversation due to another appointment, but I felt story-haunted.

As I experienced that day, if we are involved in a community of stories, then one story will eventually bump into and awaken other stories. An awakened story that is properly cared for will take an individual, a relationship, and a community in directions no one can predict. Investment in one another's stories brings wild dividends.

For days I pondered this image of "two boys playing together in a stream." I don't know its full meaning; I only know what God invited me to write. Here is part of a journal entry:

When my friend spoke about the stream, I froze. I could hear the cries of my boyhood friend, and I knew if I crossed, I'd be mauled. If I ran, I'd never be able to face him again. If I entered his persecution, I'd be pummeled. I witnessed the crime and refused to join his suffering. How often has that been my failure of fidelity in other friendships? Since then I will fight nearly to the death if a friend is assaulted, but am I willing to be a boy again and ask a friend to go play? I may be loyal now in a way I was not back then, but do I invite anyone to sit with me in the horror of that choice?

I don't know all that was exposed in my friend's simple remark, but I do know it is a story that waits for redemption. It is a story that compels me to ask: *Will I play with anyone again?* I suppose what I am most undone by is the interplay of stories. How did Asher Lev come to mind? And am I to hear in his arrival a call to the dangerous, faith-risking creativity of playing again with a new friend by a stream? If so, I am both intrigued and infuriated by this web of stories. I am again asked not only to be a child but to ask for a father who can protect me and my friends from bullies and who can help me sort through my legion of fears. Again, I am caught.

An investment in another person's story will always return to us like a boomerang, whacking us on the back of the head. The awakening whack helps us see that we "move on the margin of reality like a sleepwalker."[6] The more awake we become, the more we can play in the story we are called to write for others and that others are called to write on our behalf.

Will I receive from the wounded hands my day's portion of story, and will I bring my tears and battered questions for him to engage? Will I bring my story to the gospel and cry out for him to answer? And will I offer my broken story as a gift to others to taste and see that God is both odd and good? If I will do this, then the gift that I receive will stagger me—God's story will be my own. Your story will be mine, mine will be yours, and we all will be his.

Telling Your Story

Your stories are meant to be given away to others for their benefit. And the stories of others are meant for your benefit. What stories told to you have impacted you the most? What characteristics of God do you see revealed through the stories of others? What have you learned about yourself in the process of writing your stories and telling them in community?

postscript

Your story, like mine, will never end, not even in heaven. But your story does more than merely loop in on itself in an endless cycle of regress and return. It moves with a syncopated anarchy, a pulse and rhythm that are free of any predictable pattern, free of the typical restraints. Your story may seldom make sense to a linear mind, but still it shimmers with the distinct emblem of a Creator. Story is where we find ourselves and, every so often, God. It is where God hints at himself and invites us to see what can't be clearly seen—that he exists and intends to reward those who earnestly seek him.

Story is also where we find one another, and in the finding of another, we are confronted with the strangeness of the face that summons us to enter his or her story. If I succumb and ask, "Who are you? How did you come to be here? Where are you going? And why would you choose to go?" then I have thrown myself into the moving circle of story. I have agreed to know others and to be known by others; to know that I don't know myself and others; and to say yes to the terror of being known. I am lost and may one day be found.

How shall we end?

●

We can't deny the power of story, and Oprah Winfrey knows story like few on this earth. I weep when she invites me to vicariously accompany her to South Africa to tell a few human beings they are loved. When Oprah brings a quiet servant on stage to be honored by those who are loved by this servant, and I get to watch this humble woman receive a new minivan, a whole set of luggage, and a trip to New York, I jump out of my chair and shout, "You go, girl!" I love Oprah's love of story.

●

We also can't deny that story is personal. My friend Frank, who is a former LAPD detective, found my biological father's grave. I will visit it when I know I'm ready. I am not ready yet. I must finish Albert Camus' *The First Man* one more time before I am prepared to kneel by my father's grave and cry. But I am so thankful for my friend Frank, who survived being shot thirteen times by a gang and who now helps me remember my name when I'm not sure why God put an ex-cop and an ex–drug dealer together.

●

At Mars Hill Graduate School, we have begun a new workshop and retreat for those interested in pursuing the rhythms of story. It is another creation, another risk. Why must my belly grow in hope when I am so weary of feeding all the dreams that have been birthed? It's simple. I can't sate my hunger for story. And to follow the track of a single person's story may take me to the edge where I find God. A sighting of the Deity is worth the quest.

We're within days of selecting a new chief operating officer at Mars Hill Graduate School. I have just now been able to name the truth that, in part, I'm not looking for a COO as much as I'm looking for a father. The leading candidate is younger than I am and wiser in the ways of an organization than I am by the stretch of the stars of Andromeda. He will be a good friend, an excellent colleague, and, most likely, a lousy father. No one can father me but my fathers, and both of them died and betrayed me before their bodies were cold in the ground. But I want a father, a flesh-and-blood papa—and no one has stepped forward. I'm looking for what I know I can't require any man to be. Still, I can't deny what I desire and remain alive to the presence of my Father.

I wait for his coming, and it will be through story that he arrives.

Notes

Introduction

1. Christians customarily refer to these activities as evangelism and discipleship. But as we Christians have pursued these activities, we typically have missed the importance of wedding the stories of God with the stories of those with whom we share the gospel.

Chapter 1

The epigraph to this chapter is drawn from J. R. R. Tolkien, *The Lord of the Rings,* single-volume edition (Boston: Houghton Mifflin, 1999), 696.

1. Tolkien, *Rings,* 696.
2. Tolkien, *Rings,* 696.
3. See Genesis 1:27.

4. For most of us, the one character who is banned from real dialogue and ignored in the plot is God. Even when he is center stage, he seldom is allowed a voice or given substance as a central character. It's strange that the Creator is not welcomed as a character in our creation. In fact, in the text of your story and mine, God is both Creator and character. It's interesting that we can give him no room or voice in our play, but he always gives us a voice in his creation.

5. For more on this idea, see E. M. Forster, *Aspects of the Novel* (New York: Harcourt Brace Jovanovich, 1955).

Chapter 2

The epigraph to this chapter is drawn from Hélène Cixous, *Three Steps on the Ladder of Writing* (New York: Columbia University Press, 1993), 130.

1. Leland Ryken, James C. Wilhoit, Tremper Longman III, and others, eds., *Dictionary of Biblical Imagery* (Downers Grove, IL: InterVarsity, 1998), 582.

2. See Genesis 32:28.

3. Revelation 2:17.

4. Bill George, "Why It's Hard to Do What's Right," *Fortune*, September 29, 2003, 95.

Chapter 3

The epigraph to this chapter is drawn from Daniel Taylor, *Tell Me a Story: The Life-Shaping Power of Our Stories* (New York: Doubleday, 1996), 125.

1. Genesis 37:3-5,18-20,23-28.

2. Robert McKee, "Storytelling That Moves People," *Harvard Business Review,* June 2003, 6. Used by permission.

Chapter 4

The epigraph to this chapter is drawn from Franz Kafka, *Letters to Friends, Family, and Editors,* trans. Richard and Clara Winston (New York: Schocken, 1978), 16.

1. Ecclesiastes 3:11.
2. Margery Williams, *The Velveteen Rabbit* (New York: Bantam Doubleday Dell, 1922), 5.

Chapter 5

The epigraph to this chapter is drawn from C. S. Lewis, *Till We Have Faces* (New York: Harcourt, 1956), 249.

1. Psalm 55:12-14.
2. See Psalm 55:5-8.

Chapter 6

The epigraph to this chapter is drawn from Frederick Buechner, *Telling Secrets* (New York: HarperCollins, 1991), 32.

1. For more on this idea, see Cleanth Brooks and Robert Penn Warren, eds., *Understanding Fiction* (Upper Saddle River, NJ: Prentice-Hall, 1979), 178.
2. Isaiah 1:11,17.
3. Amos 5:21-24.

Chapter 7

The epigraph to this chapter is drawn from Hélène Cixous, *Stigmata: Escaping Texts* (New York: Routledge, 1998), 53.

1. Proverbs 16:1-4,9,33.

Chapter 8

The epigraph to this chapter is drawn from Anne Lamott, *Bird by Bird: Some Instructions on Writing and Life* (New York: First Anchor, 1995), 26.

Chapter 9

The epigraph to this chapter is drawn from Dietrich Bonhoeffer, *Creation and Fall/Temptation: Two Biblical Studies,* trans. John C. Fletcher and Eberhard Bethge (New York: Macmillan, 1959), 38.

1. John 6:53-54.
2. Genesis 16:7-8, NASB.
3. See Hebrews 12:5-6.
4. See Joshua 4:1-7.
5. Joshua 4:6-7.
6. See 2 Samuel 7.
7. Elaine Martin, "Hap-pea," abridged from www.mcilwain.org//mgam.htm, 2003.

Chapter 10

The epigraph to this chapter is drawn from Kathleen Norris, *The Cloister Walk* (New York: Riverhead, 1996), 295.

1. See Romans 8:26.
2. Psalm 139:23-24.
3. Luke 18:10-13, NIV.
4. See Matthew 18:20 and 1 Thessalonians 5:17.
5. For examples of God's repenting, see 1 Samuel 15:11,28-29,35; Jeremiah 18:7-8; 26:1-3; and Jonah 3:10. The fact that God repents opens a can of worms. How can the biblical text speak of God in language that seems to compromise his sovereign power and authority?

   But consider what Bruce Demarest, writing in Denver Seminary's online journal, says: "Scripture plainly teaches, on one hand, that God is the perfectly sovereign, omnipotent, omniscient and providential ruler who authentically relates to and suffers with his creation. Scripture also affirms, on the other hand, that humans make choices and execute actions psychologically in freedom and with personal responsibility. This is seen, for example, in the history of Joseph (Gen. 45:5-8), in Cyrus' decree to permit the Jewish captives to return to the homeland (Ezra 1:1-4), and in God's foreordination of Jesus' death on the cross (Acts 2:23). In each case human beings act freely with personal responsibility to accomplish God's predetermined will. These two poles—God's infallible will and authentic human freedom—converge in the mind of God but remain as antinomies or sub-contraries to our finite human minds." (vol. 7, 2004, www.denverseminary.edu/dj/articles2004/0300/0301.php, used by permission.)

   I could not agree with him more. However, the issue still

seems tied to the demand for clarity and precision that stories seldom require. It is an antinomy. It is baffling to our finite human
mind. Perhaps that is the intent of the author and ultimately
God. Story antinomies invite us into the shadows of the story,
compel us to plunge as far as we can go, and then invite us to
shudder with the depth we've entered and cannot comprehend.

6. See Exodus 4:10-14, NIV.
7. See Numbers 23:19; 1 Samuel 15:29; Malachi 3:6; James
   1:17, KJV.
8. See Psalm 139:16.
9. 2 Corinthians 4:17, NIV.

Chapter 11

The epigraph to this chapter is drawn from the author's personal corre-
spondence with Heather Webb regarding her insights on fasting.

1. Genesis 50:20, NASB. So said Joseph to the brothers who sold
   him into slavery and then faked his death to cover their treach-
   ery. God used their betrayal and deception to preserve first
   Joseph's life and later the lives of his family—and thus the
   nation of Israel.
2. See Isaiah 50.
3. God the Holy Spirit, like God the Father, is free of gender as we
   understand gender. Thus, it is appropriate that the Spirit is the
   Lover of all people, more than capable of wooing men, women,
   and children alike. In other words, the Spirit is perfectly suited
   to lure and to love each one of us.
4. Ephesians 4:17-20, NIV.

5. Luke 22:15, NIV.
6. See the parable of the prodigal in Luke 15.
7. Isaiah 58:6-11.

Chapter 12

The epigraph to this chapter is drawn from Lewis Hyde, *The Gift: Imagination and the Erotic Life of Property* (New York: Random House, 1979), 146.

1. Philemon 17-19.
2. See Luke 16.
3. Gabriel Marcel, *Homo Viator: Introduction to a Metaphysic of Hope,* trans. Emma Crauford (Gloucester, MA: Peter Smith, 1978), 25.
4. Matthew 25:22-28.
5. See Philippians 2:3-4.
6. Marcel, *Homo Viator,* 22.

A companion workbook is available.

The *To Be Told Workbook* gives you practical, easy-to-follow exercises for exploring and embracing the stories of your life so you can follow God into a more successful future.

Also Available from Dan B. Allender, Ph.D.

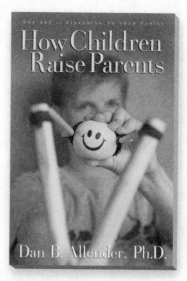

Available in bookstores and from online retailers

WATERBROOK PRESS
www.waterbrookpress.com